Empower Your Self-Love

How to Build a Positive Relationship with Yourself

JANE JENKINS

The presentation of the information is without contract or any type of guarantee assurance. The trademarks that are used are without any consent, and the publication of the trademark is without permission or backing by the trademark owner. All trademarks and brands within this book are for clarifying purposes only and are the owned by the owners themselves, not affiliated with this document.

Table of Contents

Chapter 1

Introduction

The Importance of Self-Love

Self-love is the cornerstone of a fulfilling and balanced life. It is the foundation upon which all other aspects of well-being are built, influencing our mental, emotional, and even physical health. When we cultivate self-love, we empower ourselves to live authentically, pursue our passions, and maintain healthier relationships. Without it, we may find ourselves trapped in cycles of self-doubt, negativity, and fulfillment.

The concept of self-love can sometimes be misunderstood. It is not about narcissism or selfishness but about recognizing and honoring our intrinsic worth. Self-love means treating ourselves with the same kindness, respect, and compassion that we would offer to a dear friend. It involves acknowledging our strengths and weaknesses, forgiving ourselves for past mistakes, and embracing our unique qualities.

One of the most profound impacts of self-love is its ability to enhance our mental health. When we love ourselves, we are better equipped to manage stress, anxiety, and depression. We develop a more resilient mindset, allowing us to navigate life's challenges with greater ease. Self-love acts as a buffer against the negative effects of stress, providing us with the emotional resources needed to cope with adversity.

Emotionally, self-love fosters a sense of inner peace and contentment. It allows us to regulate our emotions more effectively, reducing the intensity and duration of negative feelings. By practicing self-love, we become more attuned to our emotional needs and can address them in a healthy manner. This emotional stability contributes to our overall sense of well-being and happiness.

Physically, self-love can lead to better health outcomes. When we value ourselves, we are more likely to engage in behaviors that promote physical health, such as regular exercise, balanced nutrition, and adequate sleep. We are also more inclined to seek medical care when needed and to adhere to treatment plans. The body and mind are interconnected, and nurturing one often benefits the other.

Self-love also plays a crucial role in our relationships. When we have a healthy relationship with ourselves, we set a positive example for how we should be treated by others. We establish clear boundaries and communicate our needs effectively, which leads to more respectful and fulfilling interactions. Self-love allows us to give and receive love more freely, as we are not seeking validation or approval from external sources.

The journey to self-love begins with self-awareness. Understanding who we are, what we value, and what we need is essential. This involves introspection and reflection, taking the time to explore our thoughts, feelings, and behaviors. Journaling can be a valuable tool in this process, helping us to identify patterns and gain insights into our inner world.

Mindfulness is another powerful practice that supports self-love. By staying present and attentive to our experiences, we can respond to ourselves with greater compassion and understanding. Mindfulness helps us to break free from negative thought patterns and to appreciate the present moment. It encourages us to accept ourselves as we are, rather than striving for an unattainable ideal.

Forgiveness is a key component of self-love. We all make mistakes, and it is important to recognize that these do not define our worth. Holding onto guilt or shame can be detrimental to our self-esteem and overall well-being. By practicing self-forgiveness, we can release these burdens and move forward with a sense of freedom and self-acceptance.

Setting realistic and achievable goals is another way to cultivate self-love. It is important to challenge ourselves and strive for growth, but we must also be mindful of our limitations. Unrealistic expectations can lead to feelings of failure and inadequacy. By setting attainable goals, we can celebrate our successes and build a sense of accomplishment, reinforcing our self-worth.

Self-care is an essential practice in the cultivation of self-love. This involves taking deliberate actions to nurture our physical, emotional, and mental well-being. Self-care can take many forms, from engaging in hobbies and activities that bring us joy, to ensuring we get enough rest and relaxation. It is about making ourselves a priority and recognizing that our needs are important.

Our inner dialogue has a significant impact on our self-love. The way we talk to ourselves can either uplift or undermine our self-esteem. Practicing positive self-talk involves challenging negative thoughts and replacing them with affirming and supportive statements. This can be particularly challenging at first, but with consistent effort, it becomes easier to shift our mindset.

Gratitude is another practice that can enhance self-love. By focusing on the positive aspects of our lives and expressing gratitude for them, we can shift our perspective from one of lack to one of abundance. This helps us to appreciate ourselves and our lives more fully, fostering a sense of contentment and self-worth.

It is also important to surround ourselves with positive influences. The people we interact with and the environments we inhabit can significantly impact our self-perception. By choosing to spend time with those who support and uplift us, we can reinforce our self-love. Conversely, it is important to distance ourselves from toxic relationships and environments that drain our energy and diminish our self-esteem.

The journey to self-love is ongoing and requires patience and persistence. It is a lifelong commitment to ourselves. There will be times when it feels easier and others when it feels like a struggle. During challenging moments, self-compassion becomes crucial. Recognizing that it is okay to have setbacks and that progress is not always linear can help us maintain our commitment to self-love. Each step, no matter how small, brings us closer to a deeper sense of self-appreciation and fulfillment.

How This Book Will Help You

Embarking on a journey of self-love is one of the most transformative decisions you can make for your well-being and happiness. This book is designed to be a comprehensive guide, providing practical tools, insights, and strategies to help you cultivate a positive relationship with yourself. Whether you are just beginning to explore the concept of self-love or seeking to deepen your existing practice, this book aims to support you every step of the way.

Understanding the significance of self-love is crucial for personal growth. It is the foundation upon which your mental, emotional, and physical health is built. When you love yourself, you create a strong sense of self-worth and inner peace, which positively impacts every aspect of your life. This book will help you understand the true essence of self-love, dispelling common myths and misconceptions that may have held you back. By gaining a clear understanding of what self-love is and isn't, you can approach this journey with clarity and purpose.

One of the primary ways this book will assist you is by helping you identify and overcome barriers to self-love. Many of us carry negative self-talk, self-doubt, and past traumas that hinder our ability to love ourselves fully. This book will guide you through the process of recognizing these obstacles and provide actionable steps to address them. By tackling these barriers head-on, you can begin to heal and create a more nurturing relationship with yourself.

Building a foundation of self-awareness is another critical aspect of self-love that this book will emphasize. Self-awareness involves understanding your thoughts, emotions, and behaviors and how they influence your life. Developing self-awareness allows you to make conscious choices that align with your values and needs. Through various exercises and techniques, this book will help you cultivate self-awareness, enabling you to better understand yourself and your patterns. By becoming more self-aware, you can make more informed decisions that support your well-being.

Practicing self-compassion is a key component of self-love, and this book will guide you in integrating this practice into your daily life. Self-compassion involves treating yourself with kindness and understanding, especially during difficult times. It means acknowledging your imperfections and mistakes without judgment. This book will provide practical exercises and strategies to help you develop self-compassion, allowing you to respond to yourself with greater empathy and care.

Positive self-talk is another powerful tool for cultivating self-love, and this book will teach you how to transform your inner dialogue. The way you talk to yourself can significantly impact your self-esteem and overall well-being. This book will offer techniques to identify and challenge negative thoughts, replacing them with affirmations and positive statements. By shifting your internal dialogue, you can build a more supportive and loving relationship with yourself.

Gratitude is a practice that can profoundly enhance your sense of self-love, and this book will show you how to incorporate gratitude into your daily routine. Focusing on what you are grateful for helps shift your perspective from scarcity to abundance. This book will provide practical exercises to help you cultivate gratitude, allowing you to appreciate yourself and your life more fully. By regularly practicing gratitude, you can reinforce your self-worth and foster a deeper sense of contentment.

Setting boundaries is essential for maintaining a healthy relationship with yourself and others. This book will guide you in establishing and maintaining boundaries that protect your well-being. Boundaries help you honor your needs and values, preventing you from overextending yourself or compromising your self-respect. This book will provide practical advice on how to communicate your boundaries effectively and navigate challenging situations with confidence.

Embracing vulnerability is another important aspect of self-love that this book will address. Vulnerability involves being open and honest about your feelings, needs, and experiences. It requires courage and self-acceptance. This book will offer guidance on how to embrace vulnerability, helping you build deeper and more authentic connections with yourself and others. By allowing yourself to be vulnerable, you can experience greater intimacy and trust in your relationships.

Creativity can also play a significant role in nurturing self-love, and this book will explore ways to incorporate creative expression into your life.

Engaging in creative activities allows you to explore and express your inner world, fostering a sense of joy and fulfillment. This book will provide ideas and exercises to help you tap into your creativity, encouraging you to celebrate your unique perspective and talents.

Throughout this book, you will find personal stories and anecdotes that illustrate the principles and practices of self-love. Hearing about the experiences of others can provide inspiration and reassurance that you are not alone on this journey. These stories will highlight the challenges and triumphs of cultivating self-love, offering valuable insights and lessons learned along the way.

In addition to practical advice and exercises, this book will also emphasize the importance of patience and persistence. Cultivating self-love is an ongoing process that requires time and effort. There will be moments of progress and setbacks, but each step forward brings you closer to a deeper sense of self-acceptance and fulfillment. This book will encourage you to be patient with yourself and to celebrate your growth, no matter how small.

Ultimately, this book aims to empower you to take control of your journey toward self-love. By providing you with the tools and knowledge needed to foster a nurturing and supportive relationship with yourself, this book hopes to inspire a profound transformation in your life. You will learn to prioritize your needs, recognize your worth, and live authentically.

What to Expect on This Journey

Embarking on the journey of self-improvement can feel both exhilarating and daunting. This book is designed to be your companion, offering guidance, support, and actionable insights to help you navigate the twists and turns along the way. As you delve into this process, it's important to understand what you might encounter, how to handle challenges, and what rewards await you.

The first step on this journey involves self-discovery. You'll begin by examining your current life, identifying areas where you feel stuck or unfulfilled. This requires honesty and courage, as it often means confronting uncomfortable truths. But remember, acknowledging where you are is the first step toward where you want to be. By taking stock of your situation, you can start to map out a path forward.

As you progress, you'll encounter the need to cultivate self-awareness. Self-awareness involves a deep understanding of your thoughts, emotions, and behaviors. It requires paying close attention to your inner world and recognizing the patterns that shape your life. This book will guide you through exercises designed to enhance your self-awareness, such as journaling, mindfulness practices, and reflective questioning. By gaining insight into your inner workings, you'll be better equipped to make conscious choices that align with your true self.

One of the most significant aspects of this journey is learning to manage your mindset. Your thoughts and beliefs have a profound impact on your reality. Negative self-talk and limiting beliefs can sabotage your efforts and keep you trapped in a cycle of self-doubt. This book will teach you techniques to identify and challenge these negative thought patterns. You'll learn to replace them with positive affirmations and empowering beliefs that support your growth and well-being.

As you work on your mindset, you'll also need to develop resilience. Resilience is the ability to bounce back from setbacks and keep moving forward despite difficulties. Life is full of challenges, and your journey of self-improvement will be no different. Developing resilience involves building mental and emotional strength, learning to adapt to change, and maintaining a positive outlook even in the face of adversity. Through practical strategies and real-life examples, this book will help you cultivate resilience and stay committed to your goals.

Another key component of this journey is setting and pursuing meaningful goals. Goal-setting is an essential part of personal development, as it gives you direction and purpose. This book will guide you through the process of setting SMART goals—Specific, Measurable, Achievable, Relevant, and Time-bound. You'll learn how to break down your goals into manageable steps and create an action plan to achieve them. Additionally, you'll discover techniques to stay motivated and overcome obstacles that may arise along the way.

As you pursue your goals, it's crucial to practice self-care. Self-care involves taking deliberate actions to nurture your physical, emotional, and mental health. It's about recognizing your needs and making them a priority. This book will offer a variety of self-care practices, from exercise and nutrition to relaxation techniques and creative outlets. By incorporating self-care into your routine, you'll ensure that you have the energy and resilience to sustain your journey.

Building a supportive network is also vital to your success. Surrounding yourself with positive, like-minded individuals can provide encouragement, accountability, and inspiration. This book will offer advice on how to cultivate and maintain healthy relationships, seek support when needed, and build a community that uplifts you. Engaging with others who share your goals and values can make the journey more enjoyable and rewarding.

Throughout this process, you'll need to embrace vulnerability. Vulnerability involves being open and honest about your feelings, needs, and experiences. It requires courage to show your true self and risk being seen. This book will guide you in embracing vulnerability, helping you build deeper and more authentic connections with yourself and others. By allowing yourself to be vulnerable, you'll experience greater intimacy and trust in your relationships.

Creativity is another important aspect of this journey. Engaging in creative activities allows you to explore and express your inner world, fostering a sense of joy and fulfillment. This book will provide ideas and exercises to help you tap into your creativity, encouraging you to celebrate your unique perspective and talents. Whether through art, writing, music, or other forms of expression, creativity can be a powerful tool for personal growth.

As you navigate this journey, you'll also encounter moments of self-doubt and fear. It's natural to feel uncertain or anxious about change. This book will offer strategies to manage these emotions, such as mindfulness, deep breathing exercises, and cognitive reframing. By learning to regulate your emotions, you can respond to challenges more calmly and thoughtfully, reducing stress and enhancing your overall well-being.

Forgiveness is another crucial element of this journey. Holding onto grudges and past mistakes can weigh you down and hinder your progress. This book will guide you through the process of forgiving yourself and others, helping you release negative emotions and move forward with a lighter heart. Forgiveness is a powerful act of self-love that frees you from the burden of resentment and allows you to embrace a more compassionate and understanding perspective.

Throughout this book, you'll find personal stories and anecdotes that illustrate the principles and practices of self-improvement. These stories serve as real-life examples that you can relate to, showing that you are not alone in your struggles and triumphs. Hearing about others' experiences can offer valuable insights and inspiration, motivating you to stay committed to your path.

Chapter 2

Understanding Self-Love

Defining Self-Love

Self-love is a concept that often eludes many, trapped as we are in a world that frequently encourages self-criticism and comparison. Understanding and defining self-love is not just about feel-good mantras or indulgent self-care routines; it's about cultivating a deep and enduring relationship with oneself. Through this chapter, we will explore the multi-faceted nature of self-love and provide practical steps to help you integrate it into your daily life.

Self-love begins with self-acceptance. At its core, self-acceptance involves acknowledging and embracing all parts of yourself—your strengths, weaknesses, successes, and failures. It's about understanding that you are enough as you are, without needing to prove your worth to anyone, including yourself. This can be a challenging concept to internalize, especially if you've spent years striving for perfection or measuring your value against external standards. Start by recognizing the critical voice inside your head and gently countering it with compassion. For instance, if you catch yourself thinking, "I'm not good enough," reframe it to, "I am doing my best, and that's enough."

Another essential aspect of self-love is self-respect. Self-respect means valuing your own needs and desires and not compromising them for others. This doesn't mean becoming selfish or inconsiderate, but rather ensuring that you honor your own boundaries and principles. A practical way to develop self-respect is by setting clear boundaries with others. If you find it hard to say no, practice doing so in small, manageable situations. Over time, this will build your confidence and reinforce the idea that your needs are important.

Self-compassion is a vital component of self-love. Unlike self-esteem, which is often based on external achievements, self-compassion is about treating yourself with kindness regardless of the circumstances. When you make a mistake or face a setback, instead of berating yourself, try to respond as you would to a friend in the same situation. Offer yourself words of encouragement and understanding. According to Dr. Kristin Neff, a leading researcher in self-compassion, this practice involves three main elements: self-kindness, common humanity, and mindfulness. By integrating these elements into your life, you can foster a more compassionate and loving relationship with yourself.

Self-love also involves practicing self-care in a holistic manner. While self-care is often associated with physical activities like exercise or pampering, it also encompasses emotional, mental, and spiritual well-being. For emotional self-care, consider engaging in activities that bring you joy and fulfillment, such as spending time with loved ones or pursuing a hobby. For mental self-care, prioritize practices that calm your mind and reduce stress, such as meditation or reading. Spiritual self-care can involve anything that connects you to a higher purpose or gives your life meaning, be it through religion, nature, or personal reflection.

It's crucial to recognize that self-love is not a destination but a continuous journey. There will be days when loving yourself feels effortless and others when it feels nearly impossible. During tough times, it's important to remind yourself that self-love is a practice that requires patience and persistence. One effective way to maintain this practice is by developing daily rituals that reinforce your commitment to self-love. This could be as simple as starting your day with a positive affirmation, keeping a gratitude journal, or setting aside time each day for self-reflection.

An often overlooked aspect of self-love is the importance of self-forgiveness. Holding onto past mistakes or harboring guilt can be a significant barrier to developing self-love. Self-forgiveness involves acknowledging your mistakes, taking responsibility for them, and then letting them go. It's about understanding that everyone makes mistakes and that these do not define your worth. To practice self-forgiveness, write a letter to yourself expressing what you've learned from the experience and how you plan to move forward. This act of writing can be a powerful step towards releasing guilt and embracing a more compassionate view of yourself.

Self-love also means celebrating your achievements and recognizing your progress, no matter how small. In our fast-paced lives, it's easy to overlook our own accomplishments and focus solely on what we have yet to achieve. Take time to acknowledge and celebrate your successes. This could be as simple as treating yourself to something special or taking a moment to reflect on how far you've come. Celebrating your achievements reinforces the idea that you are worthy of love and appreciation.

Building a supportive environment is another critical element of self-love. Surround yourself with people who uplift and support you, and distance yourself from those who bring negativity or drain your energy. Your social circle has a significant impact on your self-perception and overall well-being. Engage with friends, family, or communities that encourage your growth and make you feel valued. If necessary, seek out new connections that align with your values and aspirations.

Self-love also involves being honest with yourself. This means acknowledging your true feelings, desires, and needs, rather than suppressing them to meet others' expectations or to avoid discomfort. Honesty with yourself can be challenging, as it requires a willingness to confront uncomfortable truths and make changes that align with your authentic self. Start by regularly checking in with yourself through journaling or meditation. Ask yourself questions like, "What do I really need right now?" or "What am I avoiding that I need to face?" By cultivating this habit of self-inquiry, you become more attuned to your inner voice and better equipped to live in harmony with your true self.

The Difference between Self-Love and Selfishness

Understanding the distinction between self-love and selfishness is crucial for cultivating a healthy relationship with oneself and others. Many people struggle with this differentiation, fearing that prioritizing their own needs might be perceived as selfish. However, self-love and selfishness are fundamentally different in their motivations and outcomes. Self-love is about recognizing your worth and taking care of yourself, while selfishness involves putting your needs above others to their detriment.

Self-love is rooted in self-respect and compassion. It means acknowledging your own value and treating yourself with kindness. Think of it as the foundation for how you interact with the world. When you love yourself, you set boundaries that protect your well-being and ensure that you are not depleted by overextending yourself. This self-respect allows you to be more present and available for others because you are not operating from a place of scarcity or resentment. For example, if you are constantly saying yes to demands at work without considering your own limits, you may become burned out and less effective. By setting boundaries, you maintain your energy and can contribute more meaningfully.

One of the key aspects of self-love is self-care. Self-care involves taking intentional actions to maintain your physical, emotional, and mental health. This might include regular exercise, healthy eating, adequate sleep, and engaging in activities that bring you joy. Self-care is not about indulgence or escapism;

it's about sustaining your ability to function and thrive. When you prioritize self-care, you are better equipped to handle stress and support others. Contrast this with selfishness, where the focus is solely on personal gain without regard for the impact on others. A selfish person might ignore the needs of their family to pursue their own interests, leading to strained relationships and a lack of mutual support.

Empathy is another critical component that differentiates self-love from selfishness. Self-love involves understanding and respecting your own feelings, which in turn helps you to empathize with others. When you are attuned to your own emotions, you can recognize and validate the emotions of those around you. This empathy fosters deeper connections and strengthens relationships. In contrast, selfishness often involves a lack of empathy. A selfish individual may dismiss or overlook others' feelings, focusing instead on their own desires. This lack of consideration can lead to conflicts and a breakdown in communication.

Consider the story of Maria, a dedicated teacher who always put her students first, often at the expense of her own health. Maria began experiencing severe burnout, which affected her ability to teach effectively. Realizing she needed to make a change, Maria started practicing self-love by setting boundaries, such as not taking work home and dedicating time to her hobbies. This shift allowed her to recharge and return to her classroom with renewed energy and passion. Her students benefited from a happier, more present teacher, demonstrating how self-love positively impacts others.

Self-love also involves self-forgiveness and acceptance. Recognizing that everyone makes mistakes and that these do not define your worth is essential. By forgiving yourself, you can learn and grow from your experiences without being weighed down by guilt or shame. This self-acceptance promotes resilience and a positive self-image. On the other hand, selfishness often involves a refusal to acknowledge one's mistakes or take responsibility for one's actions. A selfish person might blame others for their problems or refuse to change harmful behaviors, which can lead to ongoing issues and damaged relationships.

A practical way to cultivate self-love is through mindfulness and self-reflection. Regularly take time to check in with yourself and assess how you are feeling. Are you honoring your needs and values? Are there areas where you need to set better boundaries or practice more compassion? Mindfulness practices, such as meditation or journaling, can help you stay connected to your inner self and make intentional choices that support your well-being. This self-awareness is a cornerstone of self-love, enabling you to live authentically and align your actions with your true self.

It is also important to recognize that self-love is not a static state but a dynamic process. It requires ongoing attention and adjustment as you navigate life's challenges and changes. Be patient with yourself and understand that cultivating self-love is a journey. There will be times when you struggle or fall back into old habits, but each step you take towards self-love is valuable. Celebrate your progress and be kind to yourself along the way.

Self-love empowers you to contribute positively to the world. When you are secure in your own worth and well-being, you can give to others from a place of abundance rather than depletion. This generosity is not about self-sacrifice but about sharing your strengths and resources in a balanced and sustainable way. In contrast, selfishness depletes relationships and communities because it focuses on taking rather than giving. A selfish person might hoard resources or opportunities, creating an environment of competition and scarcity.

In cultivating self-love, it is helpful to surround yourself with supportive and like-minded individuals. Seek out relationships that nurture and uplift you, and distance yourself from those that drain or undermine you. A supportive community can provide encouragement and perspective, helping you to stay committed to your journey of self-love. Having friends or mentors who understand and practice self-love themselves can offer invaluable insights and support. They can help you recognize when you're slipping into old patterns of self-neglect or when you're veering towards selfishness, and they can celebrate your victories with you, no matter how small.

The Science behind Self-Love

Self-love is more than a feel-good concept; it has a substantial basis in psychological and physiological science. At its core, self-love is about accepting and appreciating oneself, which forms the foundation for mental well-being and resilience. By understanding the science behind self-love, we can better appreciate its importance and learn practical ways to cultivate it.

Psychologically, self-love is linked to the concept of self-esteem, which is crucial for mental health. Self-esteem refers to the subjective evaluation of one's own worth. High self-esteem is associated with a range of positive outcomes, including greater happiness, lower levels of depression and anxiety, and more robust coping mechanisms in the face of stress. When you love yourself, you are essentially building a reservoir of positive self-regard that can buffer against life's inevitable challenges.

Research in psychology has shown that self-love can be cultivated through practices such as self-compassion and mindfulness. Self-compassion, as defined by Dr. Kristin Neff, involves treating oneself with the same kindness, concern, and understanding that one would offer to a good friend. It consists of three main components: self-kindness, common humanity, and mindfulness. Self-kindness entails being gentle and understanding with oneself rather than harshly critical. Common humanity involves recognizing that suffering and personal inadequacy are part of the shared human experience. Mindfulness requires being aware of one's negative thoughts and feelings without over-identifying with them.

Studies have demonstrated that self-compassionate people tend to have higher levels of emotional well-being. For instance, a study published in the *Journal of Personality and Social Psychology* found that individuals who practice self-compassion experience less anxiety and greater emotional resilience. This is because self-compassion helps to interrupt the cycle of negative self-talk and enables individuals to respond to their own mistakes and failures with kindness rather than self-criticism.

Neuroscience also offers insights into the benefits of self-love. Brain imaging studies have shown that self-compassion activates the brain's self-soothing system, which is associated with the release of oxytocin, often referred to as the "love hormone." Oxytocin promotes feelings of warmth, safety, and connection, counteracting the stress response that is triggered by self-criticism. When you practice self-love, you are essentially engaging in behaviors that enhance your brain's ability to regulate stress and promote emotional balance.

Physiologically, the practice of self-love can have tangible health benefits. Chronic stress is known to have detrimental effects on the body, contributing to conditions such as cardiovascular disease, weakened immune function, and accelerated aging. By fostering self-love, individuals can mitigate the impact of stress on their bodies. For example, engaging in self-care activities such as exercise, adequate sleep, and healthy eating can improve overall physical health. These activities are not merely indulgent; they are essential components of a self-love regimen that supports the body's ability to function optimally.

Moreover, self-love can influence behavioral health by promoting healthier lifestyle choices. When individuals value themselves, they are more likely to engage in behaviors that protect and enhance their well-being. This includes not only physical activities but also avoiding harmful behaviors such as substance abuse or reckless behavior. The motivation to take care of oneself stems from a sense of self-worth and a desire to maintain one's health and happiness.

The science behind self-love also encompasses the social dimension of human behavior. Social psychology research indicates that people who practice self-love tend to have better interpersonal relationships. This is because self-love fosters a secure attachment style, which is characterized by healthy, trusting, and supportive relationships. Individuals with secure attachment are more capable of forming meaningful connections because they approach relationships with a sense of worthiness and confidence. They are less likely to engage in destructive patterns such as jealousy, dependency, or avoidance.

Additionally, self-love can enhance social support networks. When you value yourself, you are more likely to seek out and maintain relationships with people who treat you with respect and kindness. This, in turn, creates a positive feedback loop where supportive relationships reinforce your self-love, and your self-love enhances the quality of your relationships. Research has consistently shown that strong social support is a key factor in mental and physical health, providing another layer of evidence for the benefits of self-love.

Practical strategies for cultivating self-love are supported by scientific research. Mindfulness meditation, for example, has been shown to increase self-awareness and self-acceptance. A study published in the journal *Mindfulness* found that individuals who engaged in a mindfulness-based stress reduction program reported higher levels of self-compassion and overall well-being. Mindfulness practices help individuals stay present and non-judgmental, allowing them to observe their thoughts and feelings without being overwhelmed by them.

Another practical approach is cognitive-behavioral therapy (CBT), which has been proven effective in enhancing self-esteem and reducing self-critical thoughts. CBT involves identifying and challenging negative thought patterns and replacing them with more realistic and positive ones. By addressing the cognitive distortions that undermine self-love, individuals can develop a healthier and more accurate self-concept.

Gratitude practices are another scientifically supported method for fostering self-love. Research has shown that regularly expressing gratitude can significantly boost overall well-being and life satisfaction. By focusing on what you appreciate about yourself and your life, you can shift your mindset from one of scarcity to one of abundance. This positive outlook can reinforce feelings of self-worth and contentment. Keeping a gratitude journal, where you write down things you are thankful for, including your own qualities and achievements, can be a powerful tool in this regard.

Common Myths about Self-Love

Self-love is a concept often surrounded by misconceptions and misunderstandings. These myths can deter people from embracing self-love and reaping its many benefits. By debunking these myths, we can pave the way for a healthier, more accurate understanding of self-love, allowing individuals to appreciate its true value and incorporate it into their lives.

One common myth is that self-love is synonymous with narcissism. This misunderstanding arises from the belief that loving oneself means putting oneself above others or being excessively self-centered. However, self-love and narcissism are fundamentally different. Narcissism involves an inflated sense of self-importance and a lack of empathy for others. In contrast, self-love is about having a healthy appreciation and acceptance of oneself, including one's strengths and weaknesses. It involves a balanced sense of self-worth that does not diminish the worth of others. Self-love allows individuals to recognize their value without feeling superior or inferior to those around them.

Another prevalent myth is that self-love is selfish. Many people mistakenly believe that focusing on oneself means neglecting others. On the contrary, self-love actually enhances one's ability to care for and support others. When individuals take care of their own needs and well-being, they are better equipped to be present and compassionate in their relationships. Think of the analogy often used in air travel: put on your own oxygen mask before assisting others. By ensuring your own well-being, you are in a stronger position to help and care for those around you.

A third myth is that self-love is indulgent or lazy. This misconception stems from the idea that self-love involves pampering oneself with luxuries or avoiding responsibilities. While self-care activities like enjoying a spa day or taking a break are part of self-love, the concept goes much deeper. True self-love involves making choices that promote long-term well-being and growth. It requires discipline, such as setting boundaries, pursuing goals, and taking responsibility for one's actions. Self-love is about nurturing oneself in a way that fosters personal development and resilience, rather than merely seeking short-term pleasure or comfort.

Some people believe that self-love means always feeling positive and happy. This myth can be particularly harmful because it creates unrealistic expectations. Self-love does not mean denying or ignoring negative emotions. Instead, it involves acknowledging and accepting all of one's feelings, both positive and negative. By practicing self-love, individuals learn to process and cope with difficult emotions in a healthy way. This includes understanding that it is normal to experience a range of emotions and that feeling sad or angry does not diminish one's self-worth. True self-love allows for a full spectrum of human experience, embracing both joy and sorrow.

Another myth is that self-love is a one-time achievement. Some people think that once they reach a certain level of self-acceptance, they will no longer need to work on it. In reality, self-love is an ongoing practice that requires continuous effort and attention. Life's challenges and changes can impact one's self-perception, making it necessary to regularly engage in self-love practices. Just as physical health requires ongoing maintenance, so does mental and emotional well-being. This means consistently practicing self-compassion, self-care, and self-awareness throughout one's life.

There is also a misconception that self-love is only for people with high self-esteem. This myth can discourage those who struggle with low self-esteem from pursuing self-love. In fact, self-love is particularly important for individuals with low self-esteem, as it can help build a healthier self-concept. By practicing self-love, individuals can gradually improve their self-esteem and develop a more positive and realistic view of themselves. Self-love is not about having an inflated ego; it's about recognizing one's inherent worth and treating oneself with kindness and respect.

Some people think that self-love means avoiding criticism or refusing to acknowledge mistakes. This myth can lead to a lack of personal growth and accountability. True self-love involves being honest with oneself about areas for improvement and taking constructive criticism in stride. It means accepting one's imperfections and learning from mistakes rather than denying them. By embracing a growth mindset, individuals practicing self-love can continuously evolve and enhance their lives. Self-love is about striving to be the best version of oneself while maintaining self-compassion in the face of setbacks.

A particularly insidious myth is that self-love is only attainable through external validation. Many people believe that they need approval or affirmation from others to feel good about themselves. However, true self-love comes from within and is not dependent on external factors. While positive feedback from others can be gratifying, relying solely on external validation can lead to a fragile sense of self-worth. Self-love involves cultivating an internal sense of value that is independent of others' opinions. This internal validation provides a stable foundation for self-esteem that can withstand external fluctuations.

Another myth is that self-love is a sign of weakness or vulnerability. Some people believe that admitting the need for self-love indicates that they are somehow deficient or incapable. This could not be further from the truth. Practicing self-love requires courage and strength, as it involves facing one's vulnerabilities and working through them with honesty and compassion. Acknowledging the need for self-love and actively pursuing it is a powerful step toward emotional resilience and personal growth. Far from being a weakness, self-love empowers individuals to confront their challenges head-on and emerge stronger.

Cultural Perspectives on Self-Love

Self-love, while universally relevant, manifests differently across cultures, influenced by historical, social, and philosophical contexts. Understanding these cultural perspectives enriches our appreciation of self-love and offers diverse approaches to integrating it into our lives.

In Western cultures, particularly in the United States and parts of Europe, self-love often emphasizes individualism. Rooted in the philosophical traditions of existentialism and humanism, this perspective values personal autonomy and self-actualization. The notion that each person is responsible for their own happiness and fulfillment is central. Self-help movements and therapy practices frequently advocate for setting personal boundaries, pursuing individual goals, and fostering self-esteem. This approach can be empowering, encouraging people to take charge of their own lives and embrace their unique identities.

However, this individualistic perspective is not universally applicable. In many Eastern cultures, self-love is intertwined with communal values and collective well-being. For instance, in Japan, the concept of "Amae" reflects a sense of belonging and comfort derived from being cared for and caring for others. It emphasizes interdependence and the importance of relationships in one's sense of self. Similarly, in many Indigenous cultures, self-love is seen in the context of community and environmental harmony. The well-being of the individual is closely linked to the well-being of the group and the natural world, highlighting a holistic approach to self-care and self-respect.

In African cultures, the philosophy of Ubuntu—translated as "I am because we are"—illustrates the interconnectedness of humanity. Self-love, in this context, involves recognizing one's role within the community and contributing to the collective good. This communal approach fosters a sense of belonging and mutual support, where individual well-being is nurtured through strong social bonds and collective care.

Contrastingly, in many Latin American cultures, self-love is often expressed through familial relationships and communal support. The concept of "familismo" underscores the importance of family ties and loyalty. Self-love includes fulfilling familial duties and maintaining close-knit relationships. This family-centric approach provides emotional security and a sense of identity, reinforcing the idea that self-love is nurtured through love and support from loved ones.

In South Asian cultures, particularly within Hindu and Buddhist traditions, self-love is deeply philosophical and spiritual. The principle of "Ahimsa," or non-violence, extends to oneself, advocating for gentle self-care and self-compassion. Additionally, the practice of mindfulness and meditation fosters self-awareness and acceptance. This spiritual approach to self-love emphasizes inner peace and mental well-being, encouraging individuals to cultivate a kind and compassionate relationship with themselves.

Exploring these diverse cultural perspectives reveals that self-love is not a one-size-fits-all concept. It is shaped by cultural values, social structures, and philosophical beliefs. Understanding these differences helps us appreciate the varied ways in which self-love can be practiced and integrated into our lives.

Practical steps to cultivate self-love can draw from these cultural insights. For instance, adopting a communal approach to self-care can be beneficial. Engaging in community activities, building strong social networks, and participating in collective endeavors can enhance one's sense of belonging and support. This can be particularly helpful for individuals who thrive in social settings and find strength in collective experiences.

Incorporating mindfulness and meditation practices from Eastern traditions can also be valuable. These practices encourage self-awareness and acceptance, helping individuals manage stress and develop a compassionate relationship with themselves. Regular meditation can foster a deeper understanding of one's thoughts and emotions, promoting a sense of inner peace and well-being.

Another approach is to integrate the concept of "Amae" or interdependence into daily life. This could involve seeking and offering support within close relationships, creating a nurturing environment where mutual care and comfort are prioritized. Recognizing that self-love can be nurtured through relationships allows individuals to build stronger, more supportive connections with others.

Drawing from the philosophy of Ubuntu, one can cultivate self-love by contributing to the community and engaging in acts of kindness and service. Volunteering, helping others, and participating in community-building activities can enhance one's sense of purpose and fulfillment. This approach underscores the idea that self-love is not just about self-indulgence but also about contributing to the greater good.

Familismo, or the emphasis on family ties, can offer valuable lessons in self-love through familial support and loyalty. Strengthening family bonds, participating in family traditions, and fulfilling familial responsibilities can provide a sense of security and identity. This approach highlights the importance of family in nurturing self-love and emotional well-being.

Adopting a holistic approach to self-love, inspired by Indigenous cultures, involves considering the interconnectedness of all aspects of life. This can include developing a deeper connection with nature, practicing sustainability, and recognizing the impact of one's actions on the environment and community. By fostering a holistic perspective, individuals can cultivate a balanced and harmonious approach to self-love.

It's important to recognize that these cultural practices are not mutually exclusive. Individuals can draw from multiple traditions to create a personalized approach to self-love that resonates with their values and lifestyle. For example, one might combine mindfulness practices from Eastern traditions with the communal ethos of Ubuntu, creating a balanced approach that nurtures both individual well-being and community engagement.

Chapter 3
Identifying Self-Love Barriers

Recognizing Negative Self-Talk

Negative self-talk is an insidious force that can undermine self-esteem, erode confidence, and perpetuate a cycle of self-doubt. Recognizing and addressing this harmful internal dialogue is a crucial step towards cultivating a healthier self-perception and achieving personal growth. This chapter delves into the origins, manifestations, and strategies to combat negative self-talk, providing practical advice for beginners to transform their inner narrative.

Negative self-talk often originates from early life experiences and social conditioning. Messages received from parents, teachers, peers, and media can shape how we view ourselves. For instance, a child repeatedly criticized for their mistakes may internalize a belief that they are inherently flawed or incapable. These early impressions can solidify into persistent negative thoughts that echo throughout adulthood.

Self-awareness is the first step in recognizing negative self-talk. Often, these thoughts are so ingrained that they operate almost unconsciously, influencing behavior and emotions without our explicit awareness. To begin addressing them, one must learn to identify when they occur. This involves tuning into one's internal dialogue and noting specific instances where negative thoughts arise. Keeping a journal can be particularly helpful in this process. By recording moments of self-criticism, the context in which they occur, and the feelings they evoke, individuals can start to see patterns and triggers.

Negative self-talk typically falls into several common categories. Catastrophizing, for example, involves imagining the worst possible outcomes. A person might think, "If I don't do well on this project, I'll lose my job and never be successful." Another form is all-or-nothing thinking, where situations are viewed in black and white terms, such as "I failed this test, so I'm a complete failure." Overgeneralization involves drawing broad, negative conclusions from a single event, like "I didn't get this job, so I'll never find employment." Recognizing these patterns is crucial for addressing them effectively.

Once identified, challenging negative self-talk is the next step. This involves questioning the validity of these thoughts and considering alternative, more balanced perspectives. Cognitive restructuring, a technique from cognitive-behavioral therapy, can be particularly useful here. For instance, if someone catches themselves thinking, "I'm terrible at my job," they can counter this by listing evidence of their successes and competencies. This reframing process helps to dismantle irrational beliefs and replace them with more constructive ones.

Another effective strategy is practicing self-compassion. Often, people are much harsher on themselves than they would be on others. By treating oneself with the same kindness and understanding one would offer a friend, individuals can mitigate the impact of negative self-talk. This involves acknowledging that everyone makes mistakes and that imperfection is a natural part of the human experience. Self-compassion exercises, such as writing a letter of empathy to oneself or engaging in mindful self-kindness, can foster a more supportive inner dialogue.

Mindfulness practices can also play a pivotal role in managing negative self-talk. By cultivating a non-judgmental awareness of thoughts and feelings, mindfulness allows individuals to observe negative thoughts without becoming entangled in them. Techniques such as meditation, deep breathing, and body scans can help to create a mental space where one can recognize negative self-talk as just thoughts, rather than as definitive truths. This detachment reduces the power these thoughts have over one's emotions and actions.

Positive affirmations are another tool that can counteract negative self-talk. These are statements that reinforce positive beliefs about oneself, such as "I am capable," "I am deserving of love," or "I can handle challenges." Repeating these affirmations regularly, especially during moments of self-doubt, can help to rewire the brain to adopt a more positive self-view. It's essential, however, that these affirmations feel authentic and believable. Otherwise, they may not be effective. Personalizing affirmations to resonate with one's experiences and aspirations can enhance their impact.

Building a supportive social network is also critical in combating negative self-talk. Surrounding oneself with positive, encouraging people can provide external validation and counterbalance internal negativity. Sharing thoughts and feelings with trusted friends or a therapist can offer new perspectives and emotional support. These interactions can remind individuals of their worth and capabilities, reinforcing a positive self-image.

Additionally, setting realistic goals and celebrating small achievements can bolster self-esteem and reduce negative self-talk. Often, people set overly ambitious goals and then berate themselves for not meeting them. By breaking down larger goals into manageable steps and acknowledging progress along the way, individuals can foster a sense of accomplishment and self-efficacy. This approach shifts the focus from perceived failures to actual successes, mitigating the tendency towards negative self-assessment.

It's also important to address the underlying issues that fuel negative self-talk. This may involve exploring and healing from past traumas, addressing current stressors, or making changes in one's environment that contribute to low self-esteem. Professional therapy can be invaluable in this process, providing tools and insights to navigate complex emotional landscapes and build a healthier self-concept.

Lastly, cultivating gratitude can transform one's inner dialogue. Regularly reflecting on positive aspects of life and expressing gratitude can shift the focus from what is lacking or going wrong to what is abundant and going well. Keeping a gratitude journal, where one notes down things they are thankful for each day, can gradually reorient the mind towards positivity. This practice not only counters negative self-talk but also enhances overall well-being and contentment.

Overcoming Past Trauma

Trauma has a way of embedding itself deeply into the fabric of our lives, influencing our thoughts, behaviors, and overall well-being. Overcoming past trauma is a journey that requires patience, self-compassion, and a variety of strategies to heal and move forward. This chapter explores the multifaceted process of addressing and overcoming trauma, providing actionable advice for those at the beginning of their healing journey.

Trauma can stem from numerous sources, including abuse, accidents, natural disasters, or the loss of a loved one. Regardless of its origin, trauma often leaves emotional scars that impact daily life. For instance, someone who experienced childhood abuse might struggle with trust and intimacy, while a person who survived a severe accident might grapple with anxiety and fear in similar situations. Recognizing the pervasive effects of trauma is the first step towards healing.

One of the most critical aspects of overcoming trauma is acknowledging it. Many individuals minimize their experiences, believing that their trauma is not "severe enough" to warrant attention. This mindset can delay the healing process. It's important to accept that any event causing significant emotional distress is worthy of recognition and healing. Validating your experiences and emotions is a foundational step in the journey towards recovery.

Seeking professional help is often a necessary component of overcoming trauma. Therapists trained in trauma-focused therapies, such as Eye Movement Desensitization and Reprocessing (EMDR) or Cognitive Behavioral Therapy (CBT), can provide structured support and techniques tailored to trauma recovery. Therapy offers a safe space to explore painful memories, confront fears, and develop coping strategies. It's crucial to find a therapist with whom you feel comfortable and supported, as a strong therapeutic relationship is vital for effective treatment.

In addition to professional help, building a support network is essential. Sharing your experiences with trusted friends or family members can provide emotional relief and a sense of connection. Support groups, whether in-person or online, offer a community of individuals who understand your struggles firsthand. These groups can be a source of empathy, advice, and encouragement, reinforcing that you are not alone in your journey.

Self-care practices play a significant role in trauma recovery. Engaging in activities that promote physical and mental well-being can help restore a sense of normalcy and control. Regular exercise, for instance, has been shown to reduce symptoms of depression and anxiety, which often accompany trauma. Physical activity releases endorphins, which enhance mood and foster a sense of well-being. Additionally, practices such as yoga and tai chi incorporate mindfulness and can help individuals reconnect with their bodies in a gentle, nurturing way.

Mindfulness and meditation are powerful tools for managing trauma-related symptoms. These practices cultivate present-moment awareness, helping individuals detach from distressing thoughts and memories. Mindfulness involves observing thoughts and feelings without judgment, which can reduce the intensity of emotional responses. Meditation practices, such as focused breathing or guided imagery, can create a sense of calm and provide a mental break from the constant replay of traumatic events.

Establishing routines can also be beneficial. Trauma often disrupts a person's sense of safety and predictability. Creating a daily schedule can provide structure and stability, fostering a sense of control. Simple routines, such as a consistent morning ritual or regular meal times, can anchor you in the present and reduce feelings of chaos.

Creative expression is another avenue for healing. Art, music, writing, or any form of creative endeavor can serve as an outlet for processing emotions. Journaling, in particular, allows for the exploration of thoughts and feelings in a private, non-judgmental space. Writing about traumatic experiences can help organize thoughts, make sense of what happened, and reflect on progress over time. Artistic activities can also provide a sense of accomplishment and joy, counteracting the negative emotions associated with trauma.

Setting boundaries is crucial in the healing process. Trauma survivors often struggle with setting and maintaining boundaries, which can lead to further emotional harm. Learning to say no to situations or people that trigger distress is an important skill. This might involve distancing yourself from toxic relationships or avoiding environments that evoke traumatic memories. Establishing healthy boundaries protects your emotional well-being and fosters a sense of safety.

Healing from trauma is not a linear process. There will be setbacks and moments of intense emotional pain. It's important to approach these moments with self-compassion. Rather than criticizing yourself for not "moving on," recognize that healing is a gradual and ongoing journey. Celebrate small victories and progress, no matter how insignificant they may seem. Each step forward is a testament to your resilience and strength.

Integrating positive affirmations into your daily routine can also support recovery. Affirmations are positive statements that challenge negative thoughts and beliefs. Regularly reminding yourself of your worth, strength, and ability to heal can shift your mindset and foster a more optimistic outlook. For example, repeating phrases like "I am strong," "I am worthy of love," and "I am healing" can reinforce positive self-perceptions and counteract the negativity often associated with trauma.

Exploring new interests and activities can reignite a sense of joy and purpose. Trauma can make life feel stagnant and color less. Engaging in hobbies, learning new skills, or participating in community activities can help you rediscover passions and create positive experiences. These activities provide a sense of accomplishment and can serve as a reminder that life extends beyond the trauma.

Dealing with Self-Doubt

Self-doubt is a pervasive issue that many individuals grapple with at various points in their lives. It can manifest as an inner critic, constantly questioning your abilities, decisions, and worth. This internal struggle can hinder personal and professional growth, leading to missed opportunities and unfulfilled potential. Understanding and addressing self-doubt is crucial for anyone looking to build confidence, achieve goals, and lead a more fulfilling life.

One of the first steps in dealing with self-doubt is recognizing its presence. Often, self-doubt operates subtly, embedded in your thoughts and behaviors. You might find yourself second-guessing your decisions, downplaying your achievements, or avoiding new challenges due to fear of failure. Acknowledging these patterns is essential, as it allows you to confront the issue head-on rather than letting it undermine your confidence from the shadows.

Self-doubt frequently stems from past experiences. Early childhood interactions, critical feedback, or past failures can leave a lasting imprint, shaping how you perceive yourself. For instance, a teacher's harsh criticism or a parent's unrealistic expectations might have sowed the seeds of self-doubt. Reflecting on these origins can be enlightening, helping you understand that your self-doubt is not an inherent flaw but a learned response. This awareness is empowering, as it suggests that self-doubt can be unlearned.

Challenging negative self-talk is a powerful strategy for combating self-doubt. The voice of self-doubt often masquerades as a reasonable caution, but it is usually rooted in fear rather than reality. Start by paying attention to your inner dialogue. When you catch yourself thinking, "I can't do this" or "I'm not good enough," pause and question these thoughts. Are they based on facts, or are they exaggerated fears? Reframing these thoughts can shift your mindset. For example, instead of thinking, "I'll never be able to do this," try, "This is challenging, but I can learn and improve."

Building self-confidence is a gradual process that involves setting and achieving small, manageable goals. Each success, no matter how minor, reinforces your belief in your abilities. Start with tasks that are within your comfort zone but still require effort. As you accomplish these, gradually increase the difficulty of your goals. This approach not only builds competence but also demonstrates to yourself that you are capable of growth and achievement.

Seeking feedback from others can provide a more balanced perspective on your abilities. Often, self-doubt skews your self-perception, making it difficult to see your strengths objectively. Trusted friends, colleagues, or mentors can offer constructive feedback and highlight your accomplishments that you might overlook. Positive reinforcement from others can counteract the negative self-talk that fuels self-doubt.

Another effective method for dealing with self-doubt is visualization. This technique involves mentally rehearsing a successful performance or outcome. Athletes, performers, and business leaders often use visualization to enhance their confidence and performance. By vividly imagining yourself succeeding, you create a mental blueprint for real-life success. Visualization can also reduce anxiety, as your mind becomes familiar with the process and outcome of the task at hand.

Practicing self-compassion is essential in the battle against self-doubt. Treat yourself with the same kindness and understanding that you would offer a friend facing similar challenges. Recognize that everyone experiences self-doubt and that it does not define your worth or capabilities. When you make a mistake or encounter a setback, instead of berating yourself, acknowledge the difficulty of the situation and remind yourself that failure is a natural part of learning and growth.

Surrounding yourself with supportive and positive influences can also mitigate self-doubt. The people you interact with regularly can significantly impact your self-perception. Seek out relationships that uplift and encourage you, and distance yourself from those that are overly critical or negative. Being in a nurturing environment where your talents and efforts are recognized can bolster your confidence and diminish self-doubt.

Engaging in activities that align with your strengths and passions can reinforce your sense of competence and self-worth. When you immerse yourself in tasks that you enjoy and excel at, you provide tangible evidence to counteract self-doubt. These activities can serve as reminders of your abilities and provide a sense of accomplishment and pride.

Mindfulness and meditation practices can help you manage self-doubt by fostering a non-judgmental awareness of your thoughts and feelings. Mindfulness encourages you to observe your self-doubt without getting entangled in it. Instead of reacting to negative thoughts, you learn to acknowledge them and let them pass. This practice can reduce the power of self-doubt over time, as you become more skilled at distinguishing between irrational fears and reality.

Taking risks and stepping out of your comfort zone is a crucial part of overcoming self-doubt. Growth and confidence are often found in the space just beyond your current abilities. While failure is a possibility, it is also an opportunity to learn and improve. Embracing uncertainty and viewing challenges as opportunities rather than threats can shift your perspective and reduce self-doubt.

Maintaining a record of your achievements and positive feedback can serve as a tangible reminder of your abilities and progress. Create a journal or a digital document where you note down your successes, compliments, and positive experiences. On days when self-doubt looms large, revisiting these entries can provide a much-needed boost, reminding you of your strengths and the obstacles you have already overcome.

The Impact of Society and Media

Society and media have profound influences on our lives, shaping perceptions, behaviors, and even our sense of identity. From the moment we wake up to the subtle hum of a morning news broadcast to the late-night scroll through social media feeds, the omnipresence of media in our lives is undeniable. Understanding this impact is crucial for navigating an increasingly interconnected world where information is both a tool and a challenge.

Consider the role of traditional media, such as television, newspapers, and radio. These mediums have long served as the gatekeepers of information, deciding which stories are told and how they are framed. The narratives presented can reinforce societal norms, perpetuate stereotypes, and shape public opinion. For instance, the portrayal of gender roles in television shows from the 1950s through the 1980s often depicted women as homemakers and men as breadwinners, subtly reinforcing these roles in the minds of viewers. This has had lasting effects on societal expectations and personal aspirations.

In today's digital age, the influence of social media has surpassed that of traditional media in many ways. Platforms like Facebook, Twitter, Instagram, and TikTok are not just tools for communication but powerful engines of cultural change. They allow individuals to share their lives, opinions, and creations with a global audience, democratizing content creation and consumption. However, this democratization comes with its own set of challenges. The echo chamber effect, where users are exposed primarily to information that aligns with their existing beliefs, can reinforce biases and create divisions within society.

One significant impact of social media is the phenomenon of influencer culture. Influencers, with their curated images and lifestyles, often set trends and shape consumer behavior. While they can inspire positive changes, such as promoting healthy lifestyles or environmental awareness, they can also perpetuate unrealistic standards of beauty and success. The constant exposure to idealized images can lead to self-esteem issues and a distorted sense of reality, particularly among young people who are still forming their identities.

Moreover, the rapid dissemination of information through social media can amplify misinformation and fake news. False narratives can spread like wildfire, leading to real-world consequences such as public panic, political unrest, or health crises. The challenge lies in discerning credible sources from dubious ones, a task that requires critical thinking and media literacy skills.

Media also plays a pivotal role in shaping cultural norms and values. Films, television shows, and online content reflect and shape societal attitudes towards race, gender, sexuality, and other aspects of identity. Positive representation in media can foster inclusivity and understanding, while negative or stereotypical portrayals can reinforce prejudice and discrimination. For instance, the increased visibility of LGBTQ+ characters in mainstream media has contributed to greater acceptance and understanding of these communities. Conversely, the persistent underrepresentation or misrepresentation of certain groups can perpetuate harmful stereotypes and social inequities.

The impact of media on mental health is another crucial aspect to consider. The constant bombardment of information, the pressure to present a perfect online persona, and the addictive nature of social media can contribute to anxiety, depression, and other mental health issues. Studies have shown that excessive social media use is linked to feelings of loneliness and dissatisfaction with life. It's essential to strike a balance between staying informed and connected and protecting one's mental well-being.

Society and media are also intertwined in their influence on political landscapes. Media coverage can shape public perceptions of political candidates, policies, and events. The framing of news stories, the language used, and the issues highlighted can sway public opinion and even impact election outcomes. In recent years, the role of media in politics has come under scrutiny, with concerns about bias, misinformation, and the polarization of public discourse.

To navigate the complex interplay between society and media, developing media literacy is crucial. Media literacy involves understanding how media messages are constructed, recognizing the influence of media on beliefs and behaviors, and critically evaluating the information consumed. This skill set empowers individuals to make informed decisions, resist manipulation, and engage with media in a more balanced and mindful way.

Parents and educators play a vital role in fostering media literacy from a young age. Teaching children to question what they see, understand the motives behind media creation, and recognize the difference between reality and media representation can equip them with the tools needed to navigate a media-saturated world. Encouraging open discussions about media content and its impact can also promote critical thinking and awareness.

Moreover, individuals can take proactive steps to manage their media consumption. Setting boundaries, such as limiting screen time, curating social media feeds to include diverse perspectives, and taking regular digital detoxes, can help maintain a healthy relationship with media. Engaging in offline activities, such as reading books, spending time in nature, or pursuing hobbies, can provide a balanced and fulfilling counterbalance to the digital world.

Media creators and platforms also have a responsibility to consider the impact of their content on society. Ethical journalism, responsible advertising, and inclusive representation are essential for fostering a media landscape that promotes positive social change. Transparency in algorithms and content moderation policies can help build trust and accountability in digital platforms.

In conclusion, the impact of society and media on our lives is profound and multifaceted. From shaping cultural norms and political landscapes to influencing personal identity and mental health, the media we consume and contribute to plays a significant role in the world we live in. As individuals, we must develop media literacy, engage critically with content, and maintain a balanced relationship with media to navigate its complexities effectively.

Understanding Fear of Self-Love

Fear of self-love is a complex and deeply rooted issue that affects many individuals. It stems from various sources, including societal norms, upbringing, and personal experiences. Understanding this fear is the first step toward overcoming it and embracing a healthier, more compassionate relationship with oneself.

Imagine a young girl growing up in a household where self-deprecation is the norm. Compliments are rare, and achievements are often downplayed. She learns to be humble, but this humility morphs into a reluctance to acknowledge her own worth. As she grows, she internalizes the belief that self-love equates to selfishness or arrogance. This mindset, unfortunately, is not uncommon. Many are taught, directly or indirectly, that valuing oneself too much is undesirable or even wrong.

Society reinforces these notions through various channels. Media often portrays idealized versions of people, emphasizing physical perfection and material success. This creates a culture of comparison where individuals feel they must measure up to unrealistic standards. The constant bombardment of these images can erode self-esteem and reinforce the belief that one is not worthy of self-love unless they meet these external criteria.

Furthermore, traditional cultural values can also play a role. In some cultures, self-sacrifice and putting others first are highly valued traits. While these values foster community and connection, they can also lead to the suppression of self-worth. Individuals may feel guilty for prioritizing their own needs and desires, viewing self-love as a betrayal of their cultural or familial duties.

Personal experiences, particularly negative ones, can significantly contribute to the fear of self-love. Traumatic events, such as abuse or neglect, can leave lasting scars. Individuals who have experienced such events often struggle with feelings of unworthiness and self-loathing. They may believe that they are fundamentally flawed and undeserving of love, both from others and themselves. These beliefs can be deeply ingrained and challenging to overcome.

Fear of self-love can manifest in various ways. Some people may engage in self-sabotaging behaviors, such as procrastination, substance abuse, or unhealthy relationships. These actions reinforce negative self-perceptions and create a cycle of self-criticism and shame. Others may struggle with self-acceptance, constantly seeking external validation to feel worthy. This external reliance can lead to a fragile sense of self that is easily shattered by criticism or rejection.

Breaking free from the fear of self-love requires a multifaceted approach. It begins with self-awareness and a willingness to confront deeply held beliefs and patterns. Mindfulness practices, such as meditation and journaling, can help individuals tune into their inner thoughts and feelings. By observing these thoughts without judgment, one can begin to understand the roots of their fear and the impact it has on their life.

Challenging negative self-talk is another crucial step. The inner critic can be relentless, perpetuating feelings of inadequacy and unworthiness. Replacing negative thoughts with positive affirmations can gradually shift one's mindset. For instance, instead of thinking, "I'm not good enough," one might say, "I am worthy of love and respect." While this might feel unnatural at first, with consistent practice, it can lead to a more compassionate inner dialogue.

Therapy can also be a valuable tool in addressing the fear of self-love. A skilled therapist can help individuals uncover the root causes of their fear and develop strategies to build self-esteem. Cognitive-behavioral therapy (CBT), for example, focuses on identifying and changing negative thought patterns. This therapeutic approach can be particularly effective in helping individuals reframe their beliefs about self-worth and develop healthier, more positive self-perceptions.

Building a supportive network is equally important. Surrounding oneself with positive, encouraging people can create an environment where self-love is nurtured and celebrated. Friends and family who uplift and validate one's worth can counteract the negative messages received from other sources. Additionally, seeking out communities or groups that promote self-love and personal growth can provide valuable support and inspiration.

Engaging in activities that bring joy and fulfillment is another way to cultivate self-love. Pursuing hobbies, interests, and passions can boost self-esteem and reinforce the idea that one's happiness and well-being are important. Whether it's painting, hiking, reading, or volunteering, finding activities that resonate on a personal level can help individuals reconnect with themselves and their intrinsic value.

Self-care practices are also essential in overcoming the fear of self-love. Taking care of one's physical, emotional, and mental health sends a powerful message of self-worth. This can include regular exercise, healthy eating, adequate sleep, and relaxation techniques. Additionally, setting boundaries and learning to say no are crucial aspects of self-care. By prioritizing one's needs and protecting one's energy, individuals can create a balanced and healthy lifestyle.

It's important to recognize that the journey toward self-love is not linear. There will be setbacks and challenges along the way. However, each step taken, no matter how small, is progress. Celebrating these small victories can reinforce positive changes and build momentum. Patience and compassion toward oneself are key components of this journey. It's about embracing the process and understanding that growth takes time. Self-love is a lifelong practice, not a one-time achievement. It's about consistently making choices that honor and respect oneself, even in the face of difficulties.

Chapter 4

Building a Foundation of Self-Awareness

What is Self-Awareness?

Self-awareness is the ability to recognize and understand one's own emotions, thoughts, and behaviors, and how they align with one's values and beliefs. It is a fundamental aspect of personal growth and emotional intelligence, serving as the foundation upon which we build our understanding of ourselves and our interactions with the world around us.

Consider the story of Alex, a successful entrepreneur who seemed to have everything—a thriving business, a loving family, and a wide circle of friends. Despite his outward success, Alex often felt disconnected and unfulfilled. He couldn't pinpoint the source of his dissatisfaction until he began exploring self-awareness. Through this journey, Alex realized that many of his decisions were driven by external expectations rather than his own values. This epiphany marked the beginning of a transformative process that led him to realign his life with his true self, ultimately finding greater contentment and purpose.

Self-awareness encompasses two main components: internal self-awareness and external self-awareness. Internal self-awareness refers to the ability to introspectively understand one's inner world—emotions, motivations, and thoughts. This involves regularly reflecting on one's experiences and feelings, and understanding how they influence behavior. For example, recognizing that stress triggers irritability can help someone manage their responses more effectively.

External self-awareness, on the other hand, involves understanding how others perceive us. This aspect of self-awareness is crucial in social interactions and relationships. It requires paying attention to feedback from others and being open to different perspectives. For instance, a manager who is externally self-aware might notice that their team perceives them as unapproachable. Acknowledging this perception allows the manager to adjust their behavior to foster a more inclusive and supportive environment.

Developing self-awareness begins with mindfulness—paying attention to the present moment without judgment. Mindfulness practices, such as meditation and deep-breathing exercises, help individuals become more attuned to their thoughts and emotions. By observing these internal processes, one can identify patterns and triggers that influence behavior. This heightened awareness creates a space for conscious decision-making, rather than reacting impulsively to situations.

Journaling is another effective tool for cultivating self-awareness. Writing about daily experiences, emotions, and reflections provides a tangible record of one's inner world. This practice encourages deeper introspection and helps clarify thoughts and feelings. Over time, patterns and insights emerge, revealing underlying beliefs and motivations. For example, someone might notice that they frequently feel anxious in social situations, prompting further exploration into the root causes of this anxiety.

Feedback from others is invaluable in developing external self-awareness. Seeking input from trusted friends, family members, or colleagues can provide new perspectives on one's behavior and its impact. Constructive feedback helps identify blind spots—areas where one's self-perception differs from how others see them. For instance, a person might perceive themselves as assertive, while others view them as aggressive. Understanding these differences allows for more balanced self-views and the opportunity to adjust behaviors accordingly.

Self-awareness also involves recognizing and managing one's emotions. Emotional regulation is a key aspect of emotional intelligence and contributes to better decision-making and interpersonal relationships. Techniques such as cognitive reappraisal—reframing a situation to alter its emotional impact—can help manage intense emotions. For example, instead of viewing a setback as a failure, one might see it as a learning opportunity, thereby reducing feelings of frustration and disappointment.

Understanding one's strengths and weaknesses is another crucial element of self-awareness. A realistic assessment of one's abilities allows for personal and professional growth. Embracing strengths builds confidence and motivates further development, while acknowledging weaknesses opens the door to improvement. Self-aware individuals use this knowledge to set realistic goals and seek support or training in areas where they need to grow.

Values clarification is an essential process in self-awareness. Identifying core values—principles that guide one's behavior and decisions—provides a compass for navigating life. Living in alignment with these values fosters a sense of integrity and fulfillment. For instance, if honesty is a core value, making decisions that reflect honesty, even when challenging, reinforces self-respect and authenticity.

Self-awareness also plays a critical role in leadership. Leaders who are self-aware are better equipped to understand their impact on others, manage their emotions, and create positive work environments. They are more empathetic, open to feedback, and able to adapt their leadership style to meet the needs of their team. This leads to more effective and compassionate leadership, fostering trust and collaboration within the organization.

Cultivating self-awareness is not a one-time event but an ongoing practice. It requires regular reflection and a willingness to explore one's inner world. This journey can be challenging, as it often involves confronting uncomfortable truths and acknowledging areas for growth. However, the rewards are profound. Greater self-awareness leads to improved emotional regulation, better relationships, and a deeper sense of purpose and fulfillment.

It's important to recognize that self-awareness is a journey unique to each individual. While there are common techniques and practices, the path to self-awareness will vary based on personal experiences, values, and goals. Being patient and compassionate with oneself during this process is crucial. Growth takes time, and setbacks are a natural part of the journey. Embracing these challenges with a mindset of curiosity and learning can transform obstacles into opportunities for deeper self-understanding.

Techniques to Develop Self-Awareness

Imagine Sarah, a marketing executive who felt constantly overwhelmed by her workload. Despite her success, she struggled with anxiety and a sense of disconnection from her goals. Her journey towards self-awareness transformed her life, helping her to manage stress, make more aligned decisions, and find greater fulfillment both personally and professionally. Developing self-awareness is a powerful tool for achieving such transformations, and several techniques can guide you on this path.

Mindfulness is a foundational practice for developing self-awareness. It involves paying attention to the present moment with an open and non-judgmental attitude. By practicing mindfulness, you become more attuned to your thoughts, emotions, and physical sensations, allowing you to observe them without being swept away. One simple way to incorporate mindfulness into your daily routine is through mindful breathing. Set aside a few minutes each day to focus on your breath, noticing the sensations of inhaling and exhaling. This practice helps anchor you to the present moment and cultivates a deeper awareness of your internal states.

Meditation is another powerful technique for enhancing self-awareness. Regular meditation practice can lead to profound insights into your mind and emotions. There are various forms of meditation, but a common approach is to sit quietly and focus on your breath or a mantra. When your mind wanders, gently bring your attention back to your point of focus. Over time, meditation helps you develop a clearer understanding of your thought patterns and emotional triggers, promoting a more balanced and aware mindset.

Journaling is an effective tool for self-reflection and developing self-awareness. Writing down your thoughts, feelings, and experiences provides a tangible way to explore your inner world. Start by setting aside time each day to journal, even if it's just for a few minutes. Reflect on significant events, emotions, or decisions, and consider what they reveal about your values, beliefs, and patterns. For instance, if you notice recurring themes of stress related to work, you might explore underlying causes and potential solutions. Journaling not only clarifies your thoughts but also helps track your progress and growth over time.

Seeking feedback from others is crucial for developing external self-awareness. While self-reflection is valuable, understanding how others perceive you provides a more comprehensive picture. Approach trusted friends, family members, or colleagues and ask for honest feedback on your behavior, communication style, and impact on others. Be open to their perspectives without becoming defensive. For example, if a colleague mentions that you often interrupt during meetings, use this feedback to become more mindful of your interactions. Constructive feedback helps identify blind spots and areas for improvement, fostering greater self-awareness and growth.

Engaging in therapy or counseling can significantly enhance your journey toward self-awareness. A trained therapist provides a safe and supportive environment to explore your thoughts, emotions, and behaviors. Therapy sessions offer valuable insights into subconscious patterns and unresolved issues that influence your current experiences. Cognitive-behavioral therapy (CBT), for instance, helps identify and challenge negative thought patterns, promoting healthier behaviors and emotional responses. Therapy encourages deeper self-exploration and equips you with tools to navigate life's challenges more effectively.

Practicing empathy is another technique to develop self-awareness. Empathy involves understanding and sharing the feelings of others, which requires a high level of self-awareness. To cultivate empathy, practice active listening—fully focus on the speaker without interrupting or planning your response. Try to put yourself in their shoes and imagine how they might be feeling. This practice not only enhances your relationships but also deepens your understanding of your own emotional responses and triggers.

Body awareness is an often-overlooked aspect of self-awareness. Our bodies hold valuable information about our emotional states and overall well-being. Practices such as yoga or tai chi integrate physical movement with mindfulness, promoting a deeper connection between mind and body. During these practices, pay attention to how different poses or movements make you feel. Notice areas of tension, relaxation, or discomfort. This awareness helps you understand how your body responds to stress and emotions, allowing you to address physical and emotional imbalances more effectively.

Values clarification is a critical component of self-awareness. Understanding your core values—principles that guide your behavior and decision-making—provides a compass for navigating life. Take time to reflect on what truly matters to you. Consider moments when you felt deeply satisfied or proud, and identify the values that were honored in those situations. For example, if you felt fulfilled after helping someone in need, compassion might be a core value. Aligning your actions with your values fosters a sense of integrity and authenticity, enhancing overall well-being.

Setting intentions can also aid in developing self-awareness. Each morning, take a few moments to set an intention for the day. This could be a specific goal, such as remaining calm during stressful situations, or a broader focus, like practicing gratitude. Setting intentions creates a framework for mindful living, encouraging you to stay aligned with your values and goals throughout the day. At the end of the day, reflect on how well you upheld your intention and what you learned from the experience.

Exploring your strengths and weaknesses is another key technique for self-awareness. Conduct a personal strengths and weaknesses assessment to gain a realistic understanding of your capabilities. Reflect on past experiences where you excelled and identify the skills or qualities that contributed to your success. Similarly, consider situations where you struggled and pinpoint areas for improvement. This honest appraisal helps you leverage your strengths while addressing weaknesses, leading to more balanced personal and professional development. For instance, if you recognize that public speaking is a weakness, you might seek opportunities to practice and improve in this area.

The Role of Mindfulness

Every morning, before the hustle and bustle of his day began, John would sit quietly in his living room, legs crossed, eyes gently closed, and breathe. It was a ritual he discovered during a particularly stressful period in his life. He found that these few moments of stillness helped him navigate his day with more clarity and calm. This practice, known as mindfulness, has been a cornerstone in John's journey towards a more balanced and fulfilling life.

Mindfulness, at its core, involves paying attention to the present moment with an attitude of openness and acceptance. It is a simple yet profound practice that can transform the way we interact with the world and ourselves. By grounding ourselves in the present, we create a buffer against the incessant pull of past regrets and future anxieties. This chapter delves into the role of mindfulness, its benefits, and practical ways to incorporate it into daily life.

One of the most significant benefits of mindfulness is its ability to reduce stress. Chronic stress is a pervasive issue in modern society, contributing to various physical and mental health problems. Mindfulness helps by breaking the cycle of rumination—repetitive, negative thinking patterns that exacerbate stress. When John began his mindfulness practice, he noticed a marked decrease in his stress levels. He became more aware of his thoughts and learned to observe them without getting entangled. This detachment allowed him to respond to stressful situations more calmly and thoughtfully.

Another critical aspect of mindfulness is its impact on emotional regulation. Emotions are an integral part of the human experience, but they can sometimes overwhelm us. Mindfulness teaches us to acknowledge our emotions without judgment, creating space to understand and process them. This practice fosters emotional resilience, allowing us to handle difficult emotions more effectively. For example, when John felt anger rising during a disagreement, his mindfulness training helped him pause and breathe, preventing an impulsive reaction. This pause gave him the clarity to communicate more constructively.

Enhancing focus and concentration is another remarkable benefit of mindfulness. In a world filled with distractions, maintaining sustained attention can be challenging. Mindfulness strengthens our ability to concentrate by training the mind to stay present. During his workday, John noticed that his productivity improved as he became less prone to distractions. Tasks that once seemed daunting were now approached with a clear and focused mind. This improved concentration not only enhanced his work performance but also increased his overall job satisfaction.

Mindfulness also plays a vital role in improving relationships. By fostering a non-judgmental and empathetic attitude, mindfulness helps us connect more deeply with others. When we are fully present in our interactions, we listen more attentively and respond more thoughtfully. John found that his relationships with family, friends, and colleagues improved as he became more mindful. He was more patient and understanding, which created a more positive and supportive environment. This deepened sense of connection brought greater harmony and satisfaction to his interpersonal relationships.

Physical health benefits are another compelling reason to practice mindfulness. Research has shown that mindfulness can reduce symptoms of chronic pain, lower blood pressure, and improve sleep quality. These physical benefits stem from the stress-reducing and relaxation-inducing effects of mindfulness. John, who had struggled with insomnia for years, found that his nightly mindfulness practice helped him fall asleep more easily and enjoy deeper, more restorative sleep. This improvement in sleep quality had a cascading effect on his overall health and well-being.

Incorporating mindfulness into daily life can be done through various practices. One of the most accessible methods is mindful breathing. This involves focusing on the breath, noticing the sensations of inhaling and exhaling, and gently bringing the mind back whenever it wanders. John started with just a few minutes of mindful breathing each morning and gradually increased the duration as he became more comfortable. This simple practice anchored him in the present moment and set a calm tone for the rest of his day.

Another effective mindfulness practice is the body scan. This involves systematically bringing attention to different parts of the body, noticing any sensations without trying to change them. The body scan helps cultivate a deeper awareness of physical states and can be particularly useful for releasing tension. John found that doing a body scan before bed helped him relax and prepare for sleep. It became a cherished part of his nightly routine, contributing to his improved sleep quality.

Mindful eating is another practical way to integrate mindfulness into everyday life. This practice involves paying full attention to the experience of eating— savoring the flavors, textures, and aromas of food, and noticing the body's hunger and fullness cues. John, who often ate on the go, discovered that mindful eating not only enhanced his enjoyment of food but also improved his digestion and helped him make healthier food choices. By eating mindfully, he developed a more positive and balanced relationship with food.

Mindfulness meditation is a more formal practice that involves setting aside time to sit quietly and focus on the present moment. This can be done through guided meditations, which provide instructions and support, or through silent meditation. John found that joining a local meditation group provided a sense of community and accountability, helping him establish a regular meditation practice. Over time, this practice became a cornerstone of his daily routine, offering a sanctuary of calm and insight amidst the busyness of life.

Journaling for Self-Discovery

Emily had always felt there was something more to her life, an undercurrent of thoughts and feelings she couldn't quite grasp. It wasn't until she picked up a pen and a blank notebook that she began to uncover the depths of her inner world. Journaling for self-discovery became her daily ritual, a practice that illuminated her path and brought clarity to her emotions and aspirations.

Journaling is a powerful tool for self-discovery, offering a private space to explore thoughts, feelings, and experiences. By writing regularly, we can delve into our subconscious, uncover patterns, and gain insights into our true selves. This chapter explores the transformative power of journaling and provides practical advice for beginners looking to embark on this journey of self-exploration.

The act of journaling creates a dialogue with oneself, an intimate conversation where we can be completely honest and vulnerable. For Emily, journaling was like opening a window to her soul. She began by writing about her day, noting events and interactions. Over time, her entries evolved, becoming more reflective and introspective. She started to ask herself deeper questions: Why did I react that way? What do I truly want? These questions led to revelations about her motivations, fears, and desires.

One of the most profound benefits of journaling is its ability to clarify thoughts and emotions. Life often feels chaotic, and our minds can be a whirlwind of conflicting thoughts. Writing things down helps organize these thoughts, making them more manageable and understandable. Emily found that when she felt overwhelmed, journaling allowed her to untangle her thoughts and see things more clearly. It was as if the act of writing brought order to the chaos in her mind.

Journaling also serves as a mirror, reflecting our innermost feelings and beliefs. By regularly recording our thoughts, we can identify recurring themes and patterns in our behavior. Emily noticed that she often wrote about feeling unappreciated at work. This recurring theme highlighted an underlying issue she hadn't fully acknowledged. Recognizing this pattern prompted her to address the situation, leading to a constructive conversation with her boss and a more fulfilling work environment.

Moreover, journaling provides a safe space to process emotions. In our fast-paced lives, we often suppress our feelings, pushing them aside to focus on immediate tasks. Journaling offers a release valve, allowing us to express emotions freely and without judgment. Emily used her journal to vent her frustrations, fears, and anxieties. This emotional release was cathartic, helping her to process and move past negative feelings.

Another significant aspect of journaling is its ability to foster self-compassion. Writing about our experiences and challenges can help us view them from a different perspective, often with more empathy and understanding. Emily found that when she wrote about her mistakes and shortcomings, she was able to forgive herself more easily. She began to treat herself with the same kindness and compassion she would offer a friend, which was a crucial step in her journey of self-discovery.

Journaling can also be a tool for setting and achieving goals. By clearly articulating our aspirations and tracking our progress, we can stay motivated and accountable. Emily started using her journal to outline her goals, both big and small. She broke them down into actionable steps and regularly reviewed her progress. This practice not only kept her on track but also provided a sense of accomplishment as she saw her goals come to fruition.

To begin a journaling practice, it's essential to create a conducive environment. Find a quiet, comfortable space where you can write without distractions. Choose a journal that feels inviting, whether it's a beautifully bound notebook or a simple digital document. Set aside a specific time each day for journaling, making it a non-negotiable part of your routine. Consistency is key; even a few minutes each day can make a significant difference.

For beginners, starting with prompted journaling can be helpful. Prompts provide a starting point, easing the pressure of staring at a blank page. Some effective prompts include: What am I grateful for today? What challenges did I face, and how did I overcome them? What did I learn about myself today? These prompts encourage reflection and self-exploration, making it easier to dive into deeper topics as you become more comfortable with the practice.

Free writing, where you write continuously without worrying about grammar or structure, is another effective technique. This stream-of-consciousness approach allows thoughts to flow naturally, often leading to surprising insights. Emily found that her most profound discoveries often came from free writing sessions. By allowing her mind to wander and her pen to move freely, she tapped into her subconscious, uncovering thoughts and feelings she hadn't realized were there.

Reflective journaling, where you look back on past entries and reflect on your growth, is also beneficial. This practice provides perspective, highlighting how far you've come and what you've learned along the way. Emily made it a habit to read her previous entries at the end of each month. This reflection not only reinforced her progress but also revealed patterns and insights she might have missed initially.

It's important to approach journaling with an open mind and an attitude of curiosity. There is no right or wrong way to journal; the process is deeply personal and unique to each individual. Allow yourself the freedom to explore different styles and techniques until you find what resonates with you. Emily experimented with various methods, including bullet journaling, gratitude lists, and artistic journaling with drawings and collages. Each approach brought a new dimension to her self-discovery journey, enriching her understanding of herself.

Analyzing Personal Values and Beliefs

The quiet of the morning always provided Jason with a perfect backdrop for reflection. Over time, he realized that his decisions, feelings, and reactions were deeply influenced by his core values and beliefs. However, these guiding principles often remained unexamined and implicit. Analyzing personal values and beliefs became a transformative exercise for him, shedding light on the hidden drivers of his behavior and opening pathways to live more authentically.

Personal values are the principles and standards that dictate what is important in our lives. They guide our behavior, decision-making, and interactions with others. Beliefs, on the other hand, are convictions or acceptances that certain things are true or real. Together, values and beliefs form the foundation of our identity, influencing our views and actions. Yet, many people go through life without truly understanding these fundamental aspects of themselves.

Analyzing personal values and beliefs begins with self-reflection. Jason started his journey by setting aside quiet time each day to contemplate what truly mattered to him. He asked himself probing questions: What do I stand for? What principles guide my decisions? What am I passionate about? These questions helped him identify his core values, such as integrity, kindness, and growth. Recognizing these values was a pivotal step in understanding his motivations and aligning his actions with his true self.

One effective method to uncover personal values is to reflect on moments of pride, fulfillment, and disappointment. Jason recalled times when he felt particularly proud of his actions, which revealed values like courage and honesty. Conversely, moments of disappointment often highlighted when he had acted against his values or when external circumstances clashed with them. For instance, a job that demanded unethical practices made him realize how much he valued integrity. These reflections provided concrete examples of how his values played out in real life.

Beliefs often stem from early experiences, culture, and upbringing. Jason examined his beliefs by considering the sources of his convictions. He explored how his family, education, and societal norms shaped his worldview. This process involved questioning long-held beliefs to determine whether they still served him or if they were remnants of past conditioning. For example, Jason had always believed that success was measured by material wealth, a notion ingrained by his upbringing. Upon reflection, he realized that he valued meaningful work and personal growth more than financial gain.

To delve deeper, Jason used journaling as a tool for analysis. Writing down his thoughts allowed him to organize and articulate his values and beliefs clearly. He wrote about significant life events and how they influenced his values. This practice not only clarified his thoughts but also revealed patterns and connections he hadn't noticed before. Jason found that his value of kindness was consistently reinforced through his relationships and community involvement, while his belief in continuous learning was evident in his pursuit of new skills and knowledge.

Another powerful approach is to examine role models and inspirations. Jason reflected on people he admired and considered what qualities and values they embodied. These reflections helped him identify aspirational values that he wanted to cultivate within himself. For example, he admired a mentor's resilience and commitment to social justice, which inspired him to prioritize these values in his own life.

Confronting conflicting values and beliefs is an inevitable part of this analysis. Jason noticed that some of his values occasionally clashed, leading to internal conflict. For instance, his value of family sometimes conflicted with his value of career advancement. Recognizing these conflicts allowed him to prioritize and make conscious choices. He learned to balance his values by setting boundaries and making decisions that honored his most important principles.

An important aspect of analyzing personal values and beliefs is understanding their dynamic nature. Values and beliefs are not static; they evolve with new experiences and insights. Jason embraced this fluidity, regularly revisiting and reassessing his values to ensure they remained aligned with his evolving self.

This practice helped him stay true to himself while adapting to life's changes.

Living in alignment with one's values and beliefs fosters authenticity and fulfillment. Jason made a conscious effort to incorporate his values into his daily life. He chose a career that resonated with his passion for helping others and sought out relationships that supported his growth. By making decisions that reflected his values, he experienced a greater sense of purpose and satisfaction.

However, the journey of analyzing personal values and beliefs is not without challenges. It requires introspection, honesty, and sometimes difficult choices. Jason encountered moments of doubt and discomfort as he confronted aspects of himself that needed change. Yet, these challenges were integral to his growth. He learned to embrace discomfort as a sign of progress and used it as a catalyst for deeper self-understanding.

To support this journey, seeking feedback from trusted friends, family, or mentors can be invaluable. Jason often discussed his reflections with a close friend who provided different perspectives and insights. These conversations enriched his understanding and helped him see blind spots. Having a supportive network also provided encouragement and accountability, making the process less isolating.

Incorporating mindfulness practices can enhance the analysis of personal values and beliefs. Jason found that meditation and mindfulness helped him stay present and attuned to his inner self. These practices created a mental space for reflection, allowing him to observe his thoughts and emotions without judgment. Through mindfulness, Jason could more clearly see how his values and beliefs influenced his daily actions and reactions, helping him make more conscious choices.

The Power of Self-Reflection

Self-reflection is a powerful tool for personal growth and self-awareness. It involves examining our thoughts, emotions, and actions to gain insight into our behaviors and motivations. By regularly engaging in self-reflection, we can identify patterns, recognize areas for improvement, and make conscious choices that align with our values and goals.

Consider Emma, a marketing executive who felt increasingly dissatisfied with her job. Despite her success, she couldn't shake the feeling that something was missing. Emma began a practice of self-reflection, setting aside time each evening to journal about her day. She asked herself questions like: What went well today? What challenges did I face? How did I respond to those challenges? What did I learn about myself? Over time, Emma noticed patterns in her responses. She realized that her dissatisfaction stemmed from a lack of creative freedom and a desire to make a more meaningful impact. This awareness prompted her to explore new career opportunities that aligned better with her passions.

Self-reflection can take many forms, from journaling to meditation to simply sitting quietly and contemplating one's experiences. The key is to create a regular practice that allows for honest and open introspection. For some, this might mean starting or ending the day with a few minutes of quiet reflection. For others, it might involve a more structured approach, such as writing in a journal or engaging in guided meditation.

One effective technique for self-reflection is the use of prompts or questions. These can help focus the mind and guide the reflection process. For example, consider the following questions: What am I grateful for today? What did I do well today? What could I have done differently? How did I feel throughout the day? What triggered those feelings? How did I respond to those feelings? Reflecting on these questions can provide valuable insights into our emotional and behavioral patterns.

Another powerful method is to reflect on specific experiences or events. This involves analyzing what happened, how we responded, and what we can learn from the experience. For instance, if you had a difficult conversation with a colleague, you might reflect on the following: What was the outcome of the conversation? How did I feel during the conversation? How did the other person respond? What could I have done differently to improve the outcome? By breaking down the experience in this way, you can identify areas for improvement and develop strategies for handling similar situations in the future.

Self-reflection is not just about identifying areas for improvement; it's also about recognizing and celebrating successes. Acknowledging our achievements and strengths can boost self-esteem and motivation. When Emma reflected on her day, she made a point to note her accomplishments, no matter how small. This helped her build a more positive self-image and reinforced her sense of competence and capability.

Mindfulness is another essential aspect of self-reflection. It involves being fully present in the moment and observing our thoughts and feelings without judgment. Mindfulness can help us become more aware of our automatic reactions and habitual behaviors. By cultivating mindfulness, we can create a space between stimulus and response, allowing us to choose more intentional and constructive actions.

Emma incorporated mindfulness into her self-reflection practice by taking a few minutes each day to sit quietly and focus on her breath. She noticed how her mind would wander to different thoughts and feelings, and she gently brought her attention back to her breath each time. This practice helped her become more aware of her internal state and develop greater self-control and emotional regulation.

Feedback from others can also enhance the self-reflection process. Sometimes, we are blind to our own behaviors and attitudes, and an outside perspective can provide valuable insights. Emma sought feedback from trusted colleagues and mentors, asking them for honest and constructive feedback on her performance and behavior. This feedback helped her identify blind spots and areas for improvement that she might not have recognized on her own.

However, self-reflection requires a balance of honesty and self-compassion. It's important to be truthful with ourselves about our shortcomings and mistakes, but it's equally important to be kind and forgiving. Self-reflection should not turn into self-criticism or rumination. Instead, it should be a constructive process that fosters growth and learning.

Emma found that practicing self-compassion was crucial to her self-reflection process. When she noticed negative self-talk or harsh self-judgment, she reminded herself that everyone makes mistakes and that it's okay to be imperfect. She treated herself with the same kindness and understanding that she would offer a friend in a similar situation.

Over time, the practice of self-reflection can lead to profound personal growth and transformation. It can help us become more self-aware, develop greater emotional intelligence, and make more intentional and aligned choices. For Emma, regular self-reflection not only helped her identify a more fulfilling career path but also improved her relationships, communication skills, and overall well-being.

Self-reflection is a lifelong practice. As we grow and change, our thoughts, feelings, and behaviors will evolve, and regular reflection can help us navigate these changes with greater awareness and intentionality. By making self-reflection a habit, we can continuously learn and grow, becoming the best versions of ourselves.

Chapter 5

Practicing Self-Compassion

Understanding Self-Compassion

Self-compassion is a crucial element for personal well-being and growth. It involves treating yourself with the same kindness, understanding, and forgiveness that you would offer a friend. This concept, while simple in theory, can be challenging to implement, especially in a society that often values self-criticism and perfectionism. To fully embrace self-compassion, it's essential to understand its components and how to incorporate them into your daily life.

Consider the story of Sarah, a project manager who constantly battled with self-doubt. Despite her professional achievements, she often found herself fixating on minor mistakes and perceived inadequacies. This relentless self-criticism took a toll on her mental health and productivity. On the advice of a mentor, Sarah began to explore the practice of self-compassion. She started by learning about its three core components as defined by Dr. Kristin Neff: self-kindness, common humanity, and mindfulness.

Self-kindness involves being warm and understanding toward ourselves when we suffer, fail, or feel inadequate, rather than ignoring our pain or flagellating ourselves with self-criticism. For Sarah, this meant replacing her harsh inner dialogue with more supportive and gentle language. When she made a mistake at work, instead of berating herself, she practiced saying, "It's okay to make mistakes; I'm learning and growing."

Common humanity is the recognition that suffering and personal inadequacy are part of the shared human experience. When Sarah faced setbacks, she reminded herself that she was not alone in her struggles. Many others also experienced failures and hardships. This perspective helped her feel more connected to others and less isolated in her suffering.

Mindfulness involves being aware of our painful thoughts and feelings without over-identifying with them or suppressing them. This balanced approach allows us to observe our negative emotions with clarity and openness. Sarah began to practice mindfulness by paying attention to her thoughts and feelings without judgment. She noticed when she was being self-critical and gently redirected her focus to more compassionate thoughts.

Incorporating these elements of self-compassion into daily life requires practice and patience. For Sarah, developing a self-compassionate mindset was a gradual process. She started with small steps, such as setting aside a few minutes each day to reflect on her self-talk and actively replace negative thoughts with kinder ones. Over time, these small changes had a profound impact on her overall well-being and resilience.

One practical way to cultivate self-compassion is through self-compassionate writing. This involves writing a letter to yourself from the perspective of a compassionate friend. For example, if Sarah was feeling overwhelmed by a project deadline, she might write a letter that acknowledges her hard work and offers encouragement and support. This exercise helps shift the internal dialogue to a more compassionate and understanding tone.

Another technique is to practice self-compassion during challenging moments. When facing a difficult situation, you can pause and ask yourself, "What do I need right now? How can I comfort and care for myself in this moment?" This simple act of self-inquiry can help you respond to challenges with greater kindness and patience.

Self-compassion can also be integrated into physical self-care practices. Activities such as taking a warm bath, going for a walk in nature, or engaging in a favorite hobby can serve as acts of kindness toward yourself. Sarah found that incorporating regular physical activity, such as yoga and hiking, helped her feel more grounded and connected to her body, enhancing her overall sense of well-being.

It's important to recognize that self-compassion is not about self-indulgence or avoiding responsibility. Rather, it's about acknowledging our flaws and mistakes with understanding and a desire to improve. This balanced approach fosters a healthier and more sustainable path to personal growth. By being kind to ourselves, we create a supportive internal environment that encourages learning and development.

Research supports the benefits of self-compassion for mental health and well-being. Studies have shown that individuals who practice self-compassion experience lower levels of anxiety and depression, greater emotional resilience, and higher overall life satisfaction. These positive outcomes are attributed to the nurturing and supportive nature of self-compassion, which helps buffer against the negative effects of stress and adversity.

For Sarah, the practice of self-compassion became a transformative journey. It not only improved her mental health but also enhanced her relationships and work performance. By treating herself with the same kindness and understanding she offered others, she was able to navigate challenges with greater ease and confidence. Her story illustrates the profound impact self-compassion can have on all aspects of life.

As you embark on your journey toward self-compassion, remember that it's a skill that requires ongoing practice and commitment. Start with small steps and be patient with yourself. Over time, these practices will become more natural and integrated into your daily life. Embrace the process with curiosity and openness, and allow yourself the grace to grow and learn.

Self-compassion is a powerful tool for personal transformation. By embracing self-kindness, recognizing our shared humanity, and practicing mindfulness, we can create a more compassionate and supportive relationship with ourselves. This foundation of self-compassion not only enhances our individual well-being but also positively influences the way we interact with others and navigate the world.

Techniques for Practicing Self-Compassion

Self-compassion is an invaluable skill that can transform the way we relate to ourselves and navigate life's challenges. Integrating self-compassion into daily life involves practical techniques that anyone can adopt. These techniques help cultivate kindness and understanding toward oneself, leading to greater emotional resilience and overall well-being.

Consider the story of John, a high-achieving professional who often struggled with perfectionism. Despite his successes, John was plagued by self-doubt and harsh self-criticism. His journey toward self-compassion began with learning specific techniques that enabled him to treat himself with the same kindness he extended to others. One of the first techniques John embraced was self-compassionate self-talk. He realized that his inner dialogue was often filled with negativity and unrealistic expectations. To counter this, John started to consciously replace critical thoughts with more supportive and forgiving ones. For example, instead of saying, "I can't believe I made that mistake; I'm such a failure," he practiced saying, "Everyone makes mistakes; this is an opportunity to learn and grow."

Another powerful technique is mindfulness, which involves observing your thoughts and feelings without judgment. Mindfulness helps create a space where you can respond to yourself with compassion rather than react with criticism. John incorporated mindfulness through daily meditation practices. Each morning, he spent ten minutes focusing on his breath and gently acknowledging any negative thoughts or emotions that arose. This practice helped him stay present and respond to his inner experiences with greater kindness.

Self-compassionate writing is another transformative technique. Writing letters to yourself from the perspective of a compassionate friend can shift your internal dialogue to a more nurturing tone. John found this exercise particularly helpful. When he faced a stressful situation, he would write himself a letter offering comfort and encouragement. This practice not only helped him process his emotions but also reinforced a compassionate mindset.

Physical self-care is an essential aspect of practicing self-compassion. Engaging in activities that nurture your body can serve as a powerful reminder of your self-worth. John made a point to include regular physical activities that he enjoyed, such as hiking and swimming. These activities not only improved his physical health but also provided a sense of relaxation and well-being.

Setting boundaries is another crucial technique for cultivating self-compassion. Learning to say no to demands that overextend you and setting limits on your time and energy can prevent burnout and promote self-care. John realized that his tendency to take on too many responsibilities was driven by a fear of disappointing others. By setting clear boundaries, he was able to prioritize his well-being without feeling guilty.

Self-compassion can also be nurtured through connecting with supportive people. Surrounding yourself with individuals who exhibit compassion and understanding can reinforce your practice. John joined a support group where members shared their experiences and encouraged each other in their self-compassion journeys. These connections provided a valuable source of encouragement and accountability.

Another practical technique is to use self-compassionate affirmations. These are positive statements that you can repeat to yourself, especially during difficult times. Affirmations such as "I am worthy of love and compassion" or "I am doing my best, and that is enough" can counteract negative self-talk and foster a more compassionate mindset. John placed sticky notes with affirmations on his bathroom mirror and computer screen as daily reminders.

Engaging in creative activities can also enhance self-compassion. Activities like painting, writing, or playing music allow for self-expression and can be therapeutic. John discovered that playing the guitar helped him relax and connect with his emotions in a positive way. These creative outlets became an essential part of his self-compassion practice.

Practicing gratitude is another effective technique. Focusing on what you are grateful for can shift your perspective from what is lacking to what is abundant in your life. John started a gratitude journal, where he wrote down three things he was grateful for each day. This practice helped him cultivate a positive outlook and appreciate the small joys in his life.

Visualizing a compassionate figure can also be a powerful tool. This involves imagining someone who embodies compassion, such as a mentor, friend, or even a fictional character, offering you kindness and support. John often visualized his late grandmother, who had always been a source of unconditional love. This visualization provided comfort and reinforced his self-compassionate practices.

Incorporating self-compassion into your daily routine can be facilitated by setting regular reminders or creating rituals. For instance, starting the day with a few minutes of self-compassion meditation can set a positive tone. During this time, you might repeat affirmations or simply sit quietly and focus on your breath, allowing yourself to be present with whatever thoughts and feelings arise.

It's important to recognize that the practice of self-compassion is ongoing and dynamic. There will be times when old habits of self-criticism resurface. During these moments, it's crucial to practice self-compassionate perseverance. Recognize that setbacks are a natural part of any growth process and use them as opportunities to recommit to your practice.

As you continue to integrate these techniques into your life, you may notice subtle but significant shifts in your overall outlook. You might find that you are more patient with yourself and others, more resilient in the face of challenges, and more attuned to your needs and emotions. These changes can lead to a greater sense of inner peace and fulfillment.

Handling Mistakes with Kindness

Mistakes are an inevitable part of life, yet many people struggle to handle them with kindness. The journey of learning to respond to errors with compassion can transform not only your relationship with yourself but also your approach to personal and professional growth. Let's delve into how to embrace mistakes with kindness, turning them into opportunities for learning and self-improvement.

Consider the story of Emma, an accomplished graphic designer known for her creativity and attention to detail. Despite her skills, she often found herself paralyzed by the fear of making mistakes. Every misstep, no matter how small, would spiral into harsh self-criticism, affecting her confidence and productivity. Emma's breakthrough came when she began to view mistakes not as failures but as integral steps in her learning process.

One of the first steps in handling mistakes with kindness is to reframe your perception of them. Instead of seeing mistakes as a reflection of your inadequacies, view them as opportunities for growth and learning. Emma started keeping a journal where she documented her mistakes, not with a sense of failure, but with curiosity about what she could learn from each experience. This simple shift in perspective made her more open to experimentation and innovation in her work, ultimately enhancing her creativity.

Acknowledging the universality of mistakes is another crucial aspect. Everyone, regardless of their level of expertise or success, makes mistakes. This shared human experience can foster a sense of connection and reduce the isolation that often accompanies self-criticism. Emma found solace in talking to her colleagues about their experiences with mistakes. These conversations revealed that even the most seasoned professionals faced similar challenges, which helped her feel less alone and more compassionate toward herself.

Practicing self-compassionate self-talk is a powerful technique for handling mistakes with kindness. When you make a mistake, pay attention to your inner dialogue. Replace harsh, critical thoughts with supportive and forgiving ones. For instance, instead of saying, "I can't believe I messed up again; I'm so incompetent," try saying, "It's okay to make mistakes; this is an opportunity to learn and grow." Emma practiced this technique by writing down her self-critical thoughts and then rephrasing them into more compassionate statements. Over time, this helped her develop a kinder inner voice that supported her through challenging times.

Mindfulness plays a pivotal role in handling mistakes with kindness. By being present and fully experiencing the moment, you can observe your thoughts and emotions without judgment. This awareness allows you to respond to mistakes with compassion rather than react with self-criticism. Emma incorporated mindfulness into her daily routine through meditation and mindful breathing exercises. These practices helped her stay grounded and approach mistakes with a calm and compassionate mindset.

Seeking feedback in a constructive manner can also help you handle mistakes with kindness. Instead of avoiding feedback out of fear of criticism, view it as a valuable tool for growth. Emma started to actively seek feedback from her peers and mentors, asking specific questions about how she could improve. This proactive approach not only provided her with actionable insights but also reinforced her commitment to learning and self-improvement.

Another technique is to practice self-forgiveness. Holding onto guilt and shame over past mistakes can hinder your ability to move forward. Forgiving yourself is essential for letting go and focusing on the future. Emma found that writing forgiveness letters to herself was a therapeutic way to release negative emotions. In these letters, she acknowledged her mistakes, expressed understanding and compassion for herself, and affirmed her commitment to learning and growing from the experience.

Creating a supportive environment is also key. Surround yourself with people who encourage and uplift you, especially during times of difficulty. Emma joined a professional group where members shared their challenges and successes. This supportive network provided her with encouragement and reminded her that mistakes are a natural part of the learning process.

Incorporating a growth mindset is another effective strategy. A growth mindset, as popularized by psychologist Carol Dweck, is the belief that abilities and intelligence can be developed through dedication and hard work. Embracing a growth mindset encourages you to see mistakes as opportunities to develop your skills. Emma started to view each project as a chance to learn and improve, rather than as a test of her abilities. This shift in mindset made her more resilient and less fearful of making mistakes.

Engaging in self-care activities is essential for maintaining a compassionate approach to mistakes. Taking care of your physical, emotional, and mental well-being can help you handle stress and setbacks more effectively. Emma made a point to regularly engage in activities that brought her joy and relaxation, such as yoga, painting, and spending time in nature. These self-care practices helped her stay balanced and approach mistakes with a clear and compassionate mind.

Reflecting on past successes can also bolster your confidence and resilience. Reminding yourself of times when you overcame challenges or learned from mistakes can provide valuable perspective and encouragement. Emma created a "success board" where she posted notes and reminders of her achievements and positive feedback. This visual representation of her successes served as a powerful reminder of her capabilities and potential.

Finally, practicing gratitude can enhance your ability to handle mistakes with kindness. Focusing on what you are grateful for can shift your mindset from negativity to positivity, making it easier to approach mistakes with a compassionate attitude. Emma began a daily gratitude journal, where she noted three things she was grateful for each day. This practice helped her maintain a positive outlook, even when she faced setbacks.

The Benefits of Self-Compassion

Imagine standing before a mirror and seeing not just your reflection, but a friend who deserves kindness and understanding. This simple shift in perspective embodies the essence of self-compassion, a transformative practice that can profoundly improve your emotional well-being and overall quality of life. Self-compassion involves treating yourself with the same care and concern you would offer to a loved one facing difficult times. It's about recognizing your own suffering, being kind to yourself, and understanding that imperfection is a shared human experience.

One of the most significant benefits of self-compassion is its impact on mental health. Research consistently shows that individuals who practice self-compassion experience lower levels of anxiety and depression. This is because self-compassion helps to temper the harsh self-criticism that often exacerbates mental health issues. Instead of berating themselves for perceived failures, self-compassionate individuals acknowledge their pain and offer themselves comfort. This approach not only alleviates immediate distress but also builds resilience against future stressors.

Consider the case of Sarah, a young professional who was struggling with overwhelming stress due to her demanding job. She often found herself ruminating over mistakes and feeling inadequate. When Sarah learned about self-compassion, she started practicing it by taking a few moments each day to acknowledge her hard work, regardless of the outcomes. This small change had a profound effect on her mental state, reducing her anxiety and helping her approach challenges with a clearer, calmer mind.

Self-compassion also enhances emotional regulation. People who practice self-compassion are better equipped to manage their emotions because they do not amplify their suffering with self-judgment. Instead, they recognize their feelings and respond with understanding and care. This ability to regulate emotions is crucial in maintaining healthy relationships, both personal and professional. By being gentle with themselves, self-compassionate individuals can navigate conflicts and setbacks more effectively, without being overwhelmed by negative emotions.

In addition to mental health benefits, self-compassion fosters a growth mindset. When you approach your mistakes and shortcomings with kindness, you create a safe space for learning and growth. This mindset encourages you to take risks and embrace new challenges, knowing that failure is a part of the learning process and not a reflection of your worth. For instance, Tom, a software developer, used to avoid taking on complex projects for fear of making mistakes. After embracing self-compassion, he began to view these projects as opportunities to learn and improve. This shift not only enhanced his skills but also increased his job satisfaction and career prospects.

Physical health can also improve with the practice of self-compassion. Chronic stress and self-criticism can lead to various health problems, including cardiovascular issues and weakened immune function. By reducing stress and promoting a positive outlook, self-compassion can lead to better health outcomes. Studies have shown that self-compassionate individuals tend to engage in healthier behaviors, such as regular exercise, balanced eating, and adequate sleep. These behaviors contribute to overall well-being and longevity.

Moreover, self-compassion can improve interpersonal relationships. When you are kind to yourself, it becomes easier to extend that kindness to others. Self-compassionate individuals are more likely to exhibit empathy and understanding in their interactions, fostering deeper and more meaningful connections. This is because they recognize the shared human experience of suffering and imperfection, which enhances their ability to relate to others. Jane, a teacher, noticed that her relationships with her students improved significantly when she practiced self-compassion. By being patient and understanding with herself, she found it easier to be patient and understanding with her students, creating a more supportive and productive learning environment.

Another profound benefit of self-compassion is its ability to enhance self-esteem. Traditional self-esteem is often contingent on external achievements and comparisons with others, which can be unstable and fleeting. In contrast, self-compassion provides a stable foundation for self-worth that is not dependent on external validation. It allows you to value yourself simply for being human, with all your strengths and weaknesses. This intrinsic sense of worth fosters a positive self-image and resilience against external criticism and setbacks.

Practicing self-compassion also leads to increased motivation and productivity. Contrary to the belief that self-criticism is necessary for high performance, studies have shown that self-compassionate individuals are more motivated and productive. This is because they are driven by a desire for self-improvement rather than a fear of failure. They are more likely to set realistic goals, persist in the face of difficulties, and bounce back from setbacks. Mark, an entrepreneur, found that his productivity soared when he replaced his self-critical inner dialogue with self-compassionate encouragement. This not only improved his work performance but also his overall satisfaction and sense of accomplishment.

Incorporating self-compassion into your daily life involves several practical steps. First, start by becoming aware of your inner dialogue. Notice when you are being self-critical and consciously replace those thoughts with kinder, more supportive ones. This might feel unnatural at first, but with practice, it becomes easier. Second, treat yourself as you would treat a friend. When faced with a mistake or failure, ask yourself what you would say to a friend in the same situation and apply that same kindness and understanding to yourself. This shift in perspective can help you develop a more compassionate inner voice.

Self-Compassion Exercises

Imagine waking up each morning with the intention to treat yourself with the same kindness and understanding you would offer to a dear friend. This mindset lays the foundation for practicing self-compassion, a powerful tool that can significantly enhance your emotional well-being. To cultivate self-compassion, incorporating specific exercises into your daily routine can be incredibly beneficial. These exercises are designed to help you become more aware of your inner dialogue, foster a gentler approach to self-criticism, and build resilience in the face of life's challenges.

One of the most effective self-compassion exercises is the "Self-Compassion Break." This simple yet profound practice can be done anywhere, anytime you feel stressed or overwhelmed. Begin by taking a deep breath and acknowledging your feelings. Say to yourself, "This is a moment of suffering." This step is crucial because it validates your experience and brings mindful awareness to your current state. Next, remind yourself that suffering is a part of life by saying, "Suffering is a part of the human experience." This helps to normalize your feelings and connect you to the broader human condition. Finally, place your hand over your heart and offer yourself words of kindness and support, such as, "May I be kind to myself in this moment." This gesture of self-care can be incredibly soothing and grounding.

Another powerful exercise is "Loving-Kindness Meditation." This practice involves silently repeating phrases that express good wishes towards yourself and others. Start by finding a quiet place to sit comfortably. Close your eyes and take a few deep breaths to center yourself. Begin by directing kind and loving thoughts towards yourself. You might say, "May I be happy. May I be healthy. May I be safe. May

I live with ease." Repeat these phrases slowly and mindfully. After a few minutes, expand your focus to include others, starting with loved ones and gradually extending to all beings. This meditation not only fosters self-compassion but also cultivates a sense of connection and empathy towards others.

"Self-Compassionate Letter Writing" is another valuable exercise. This involves writing a letter to yourself from the perspective of a compassionate friend. Think about a situation that is causing you distress or self-criticism. Imagine a dear friend who understands you deeply and loves you unconditionally. Write a letter from this friend's perspective, offering you words of kindness, understanding, and support. This exercise can help shift your perspective and reduce harsh self-judgment. It can also provide a tangible reminder of your commitment to self-compassion, which you can revisit whenever you need encouragement.

"Mirror Work" is a practice that involves looking at yourself in the mirror and speaking kindly to yourself. This exercise can be particularly challenging, as it directly confronts any negative self-image you may hold. Stand in front of a mirror, make eye contact with yourself, and say affirmations such as, "I am worthy of love and kindness," or "I accept myself as I am." This practice can help you develop a more compassionate and accepting relationship with yourself.

Engaging in "Mindful Self-Compassion Journal" is another effective way to nurture self-compassion. Set aside time each day to write about your experiences, focusing on how you treated yourself in moments of difficulty. Reflect on your inner dialogue and how you might bring more kindness and understanding to these moments. Journaling can help you become more aware of your patterns of self-criticism and develop a more compassionate inner voice. It also provides a safe space to explore your emotions and process your experiences.

"Compassionate Body Scan" is a mindfulness exercise that involves bringing attention to different parts of your body with a sense of kindness and curiosity. Lie down in a comfortable position and close your eyes. Slowly bring your attention to each part of your body, starting from your toes and moving up to your head. As you focus on each area, notice any tension or discomfort without judgment. Instead of trying to change anything, simply offer yourself compassion for whatever you are experiencing. This practice can help you develop a more compassionate relationship with your body and encourage you to listen to its needs.

"Gratitude Practice" is closely related to self-compassion and involves regularly reflecting on the things you appreciate about yourself. Each day, take a few minutes to write down three things you are grateful for in your life. Make sure to include at least one thing that you appreciate about yourself, such as a personal quality or a kind act you performed. This exercise can help shift your focus from self-criticism to self-appreciation and foster a more positive and compassionate self-view.

"Affirmation Cards" are a practical tool for reinforcing self-compassion throughout your day. Write down positive affirmations on small cards and place them in locations where you will see them regularly, such as your bathroom mirror, your desk, or your wallet. Examples of affirmations include, "I am enough," "I am doing my best," and "I deserve kindness." These visual reminders can help keep self-compassion at the forefront of your mind and provide a boost of encouragement whenever you need it.

"Guided Imagery" is another exercise that can help cultivate self-compassion. This involves visualizing a place where you feel completely safe, relaxed, and at peace. Close your eyes and imagine yourself in this place. It could be a real location you've visited or a completely imagined one. As you visualize this safe haven, allow yourself to fully experience the feelings of comfort and security it brings. Use this imagery as a mental retreat whenever you feel overwhelmed or self-critical. The practice can create a mental buffer against stress and enhance your ability to offer yourself compassion in difficult moments.

www.ingramcontent.com/pod-product-compliance
Lightning Source LLC
Chambersburg PA
CBHW072023150726
47999CB00002B/754